THE ROMANS SPEAK FOR THEMSELVES BOOK II

SELECTIONS FROM LATIN LITERATURE FOR SECOND YEAR STUDENTS

by

Donald Benander, Arthur Downey, Mary Gardner, Anita Jog,
Marjorie Keeley, Kathleen McCarthy, and Andrew Schacht

Edited by

Gilbert Lawall

Longman

The Romans Speak for Themselves, Book II

Longman, 10 Bank Street, White Plains, NY 10606

Executive editor: Lyn McLean
Cover design: Charlene Felker
Cover photo: Alinari/Art Resource
Photo research: Aerin Csigay
Production supervisor: Eduardo Castillo

ISBN 0-8013-0268-4

8 9 10–CRW–99 98

Photo Credits and Sources

Page 3: From *Pompeii: Nowadays and 2000 Years Ago* by Alberto C. Carpiceci, © 1977 by Bonechi. Page 5: The Bettmann Archive. Page 7: The Mansell Collection. Page 8: From *Houses, Villas and Palaces in the Roman World* by A. G. McKay, © 1975 by Thames and Hudson. Page 9: Reprinted by permission of Thames and Hudson, Ltd. Page 18: The Mansell Collection. Page 27: The Bettmann Archive. Page 41: The Mansell Collection. Page 43: Alinari/Art Resource, NY. Page 44 and 45: Alinari/Art Resource, NY. Page 54: Scala/Art Resource, NY. Page 58: Alinari/Art Resource, NY. Page 62: From *Rome: Nowadays and 2000 Years Ago* by Alberto C. Carpiceci, © by Bonechi. Page 67: The Mansell Collection. Page 74: Alinari/Art Resource, NY. Page 75: Scala/Art Resource, NY. Page 77: From *Orbis Pictus Latinus* by Hermann Koller, © 1976, 1983 by Artemis Verlag Zurich and München.

ACKNOWLEDGMENTS

The chapters in this book were written by graduate students in the program leading to a Master of Arts in Teaching Latin and Classical Humanities at the University of Massachusetts at Amherst; they were written as partial fulfillment of the requirements of Latin 608, Teaching Latin Literature, taught by Professor Gilbert Lawall in spring semester, 1986. These students were Donald Benander, Arthur Downey, Mary Gardner, Anita Jog, Marjorie Keeley, Kathleen McCarthy, and Andrew Schacht.

The materials were revised in 1986 by Donald Benander, Latin teacher and Head of the Foreign Language Department at Chicopee High School, Chicopee, Massachusetts. Professor Conrad Barrett of California State University, Long Beach, and David Perry of Rye High School, Rye, New York, served as consultants in the preparation of this edition and made numerous useful suggestions that have been incorporated into the lessons.

During the spring semester, 1988, Marjorie Keeley helped in many ways with preparation of the final manuscript, including compilation of the vocabulary at the end of this book. She also wrote the translations and offered many suggestions that have been included in the teacher's handbook. The editor, Gilbert Lawall, wishes to thank all those who have contributed to this book.

CONTENTS

PREFACE FOR STUDENTS

In this book you will find eight passages from Latin authors chosen to accompany the cultural topics in ECCE ROMANI, Book II. All of the authors lived in the ancient Roman world. Each passage has been adapted so that it may be read at a designated point in the course of your learning of Latin from the ECCE ROMANI series. The passages are drawn from some of the greatest and most interesting Roman authors, such as Seneca, Juvenal, Petronius, and Augustine, and cover a wide variety of topics from Roman houses to education, the gladiatorial shows in the arena, and a unique Roman wedding.

We have provided a number of features that will help you in your encounter with what these Romans had to say.

1. Each chapter begins with a brief introduction that will orient you to the topic of the Latin passage and provide some background and context for your reading of the Latin.
2. On the page opposite each segment of the passage is a vocabulary list that gives all of the words that you have not yet met in your reading in ECCE ROMANI.
3. Beneath each passage on the right-hand page you will find comprehension questions that are designed to lead you to an understanding of what the author is saying in the passage. These questions will help you comprehend and translate the Latin.
4. We then provide you with a copy of the entire passage without vocabulary but with questions that invite discussion of the passage or with suggestions of other activities that will help bring the passage alive as an actual communication from a Latin writer.

As you use this book, focus on the Latin. Listen to what the Romans had to say about themselves and about the world in which they lived. Let the Romans speak for themselves, but listen carefully to their voices. Let your reading of the following passages be an enjoyable, enriching encounter with inhabitants of a world distant from us in time and space—with people who were very different from us yet share many of our thoughts and feelings. Enjoy your encounter with them!

1
BUILDINGS
FOR DIFFERENT RANKS
OF SOCIETY

Vitruvius, *On Architecture* VI.5.1–2

(After Chapter 29)

INTRODUCTION

Roman houses were not all identical in pattern, size, and purpose. You are familiar with the **domus** and the **īnsula**, but in addition there were houses that combined features of both or added rooms to suit the needs and tastes of the owners. Houses built in this way accommodated not just the family but also the business or politics with which the family was involved.

The following passage, taken from a book on architecture by the Roman architect Vitruvius, gives an idea of what a Roman might look for in a house, as determined by his occupation and his social standing. Vitruvius' book, written in the late first century B.C., includes technical information about the construction of buildings and comments on the social functions of architecture. In the following selection, Vitruvius defines the functions of various parts of the house and suggests why they are useful to one or another social group in Rome. In passages I and II, he distinguishes between rooms that are only for the family's use (the ones present in all homes) and those that are for receiving daytime guests or conducting business. The latter rooms will vary according to the needs of the family's business and its social standing. Then in passages III and IV, Vitruvius lists various occupations and the types of houses they require.

1 **animadvertō, animadvertere, animadvertī, animadversus,** *to notice, pay attention to*
    prīvātus, -a, -um, *private*
2 **loca, -ōrum,** n. pl., *places, rooms*
    proprius, -a, -um + dat., *proper for, private to*
    patribus familiārum, *for/to the heads of households*
3 **commūnis, -is, -e,** *common, shared*
    extrāneus, -ī, m., *outsider, stranger*
4 **id est,** *that is, for example*
5 **trīclīnium, -ī,** n., *dining room*
    balneae, -ārum, f. pl., *baths*
    cēterī, -ae, -a, pl., *the rest, the other*
    huius modī, *of this kind*

VITRUVIUS, *ON ARCHITECTURE* VI.5.1–2

I.

1   Nunc etiam necesse est animadvertere quōmodo in prīvātīs aedi-
2   ficiīs dēbeās aedificāre loca propria patribus familiārum et quōmodo
3   loca commūnia cum extrāneīs. Nam in haec quae propria patribus
4   familiārum sunt nēmō potest intrāre nisi invītātus, id est in cubicula,
5   trīclīnia, balneās, et cētera loca huius modī.

Comprehension Questions

1. How does Vitruvius identify the two types of spaces or rooms that
    he proposes to discuss? (2–3)
2. Who can enter the rooms that are **propria patribus familiārum**?
    (4)
3. What three types of rooms of this kind does Vitruvius name? (4–5)

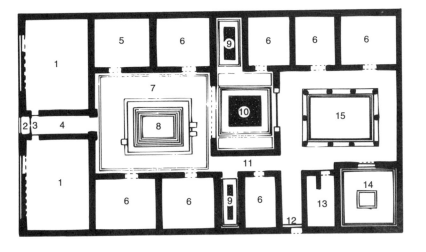

1. **tabernae** (shops)
2. **vestibulum** (entrance)
3. **iānua** (double door)
4. **faucēs** (entrance passage)
5. **cella** (room for doorkeeper)
6. **cubicula** (bedrooms)
7. **cavaedium** or **ātrium** (inner court or hall)
8. **compluvium** and **impluvium** (roof opening and tank)
9. **āla** (alcove)
10. **tablīnum** (study)
11. **andrōn** (passage)
12. **postīcum** (servants' entrance)
13. **culīna** (kitchen)
14. **trīclīnium** (dining room)
15. **peristȳlium** (garden)

Plan of a Pompeian house

6 **commūnis, -is, -e**, *common, shared*
   autem, conj., *however, but*
   loca, -ōrum, n. pl., *places, rooms*
   populus, -ī, m., *people, common people*
7 **vestibulum, -ī**, n., *entrance passage*
   cavaedium, -ī, n., *inner court, atrium*
   peristȳlium, -ī, n., *peristyle* (courtyard and garden surrounded with a colonnade)
8 **cēterī, -ae, -a**, pl., *the rest, the other*
   huius modī, *of this kind*
   commūnī fortūnā, ablative of description, *of ordinary means*
9 **necessārius, -a, -um**, *necessary, needed*
   nec, conj., *nor*
10 **in aliīs . . . vīsitandō**, *by visiting/paying their respects at the homes of others*
   officia praestant, *they perform their duties*
   ab aliīs vīsitantur, *they are visited by others*

II.

6   Commūnia autem sunt ea loca, in quae hominēs dē populō, etiam
7   nōn invītātī, possunt venīre, id est vestibula, cavaedium, peristȳlia,
8   et cētera loca huius modī. Igitur eīs hominibus, quī commūnī
9   fortūnā sunt, nōn necessāria sunt magnifica vestibula nec tablīna
10   neque ātria, quod in aliīs officia praestant vīsitandō neque ab aliīs
11   vīsitantur.

Comprehension Questions

4. How are the **loca commūnia** defined? (6–7)
5. What three types of rooms of this sort does Vitruvius name? (7)
6. What kinds of rooms do men of ordinary means not need? (9–10)
7. Why do men of ordinary means not need such rooms? (10–11)

Atrium of a wealthy man's house where clients would be received

12 frūctus, -ūs, m., *fruit, produce*
    serviō, -īre, -īvī, -ītus + dat., *to serve;* here, *to deal in*
    vestibulum, -ī, n., *entrance passage*
    stabulum, -ī, n., *stable* (for animals)
13 aedēs, aedis, gen. pl., aedium, f., *house*
    crypta, -ae, f., *underground storage room*
    horreum, -ī, n., *room for storing grain*
    apothēca, -ae, f., *store room* (especially for wine; often located just under the roof to
        collect smoke)
14 cēterī, -ae, -a, pl., *the rest, the other.* Supply loca, *rooms.*
    servent: from servō, -āre, -āvī, -ātus, *to preserve,* not serviō (see line 12)
    magis quam, *more than, rather than*
    ēlegantia, -ae, f., *refinement, luxury*
    addō, addere, addidī, additus, *to add*
    item, adv., *similarly, likewise*
15 faenerātor, faenerātōris, m., *money lender, banker*
    pūblicānus, -ī, m., *tax collector*
    īnsidiae, -ārum, f. pl., *ambush, attack, robbery*
    tūtus, -a, -um, *safe*
16 conveniunt + dat., *are suitable for, appropriate to*
    forēnsis, forēnsis, gen. pl., forēnsium, m., *public speaker, advocate, lawyer*
    spatiōsus, -a, -um, *roomy, spacious*

III.

12   Hominēs quī frūctibus rūsticīs serviunt in vestibulīs stabula et
13   tabernās facere dēbent; in aedibus cryptās, horrea, apothēcās et
14   cētera quae frūctūs servent magis quam ēlegantiam addant. Item
15   faenerātōribus et pūblicānīs loca magna et pulchra et ab īnsidiīs tūta
16   conveniunt, forēnsibus et ōrātōribus ēlegantia et spatiōsa loca, in
17   quibus multōs hominēs excipere possunt.

Comprehension Questions

   8. What people need to build stables and shops at the entrances of
      their homes? (12–13)
   9. What do these people need to build inside their homes? (13–14)
  10. What is the purpose of these rooms? (14)
  11. To what do these rooms *not* need to contribute? (14)
  12. How does Vitruvius describe the rooms needed by money lenders
      and tax collectors? (15–16)
  13. How does Vitruvius describe the rooms needed by lawyers and
      public speakers? (16)
  14. Why do they need such rooms? (16–17)

A butcher's shop

18 **nōbilis, nōbilis**, gen. pl., **nōbilium**, m., *nobleman, aristocrat* (in Rome, a man whose ancestors had held high office)
    honor, honōris, m., *high political/civic office*
    magistrātus, -ūs, m., *high political/civic office*
    gerō, gerere, gessī, gestus, *to hold* (political/civic office)
19 **vestibulum, -ī**, n., *entrance passage*
    rēgālis, -is, -e, *regal, royal*
    altus, -a, -um, *high, lofty*
    peristȳlium, -ī, n., *peristyle* (courtyard and garden surrounded with a colonnade)
    ambulātiō, ambulātiōnis, f., *walkway* (either covered or uncovered)
20 **bibliothēca, -ae**, f., *library*
    basilica, -ae, f., *large room/hall with a double colonnade* (suitable for use as a court of law)
    similis, -is, -e + dat., *similar (to)*
21 **pūblicus, -a, -um**, *public*
    cōnsilium, -ī, n., *plan, deliberation, consultation*
22 **prīvātus, -a, -um**, *private*
    iūdicium, -ī, n., *judgment, trial*
    cōnficiō, cōnficere, cōnfēcī, cōnfectus, *to accomplish, finish, conduct*

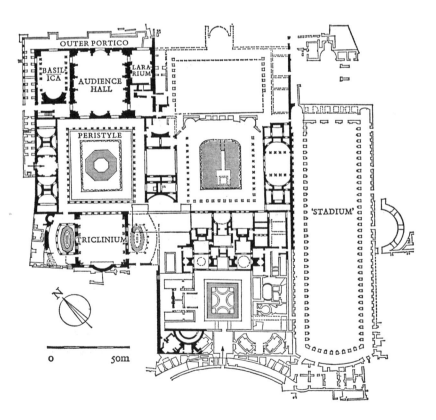

Plan of the Emperor Domitian's palace on the Palatine Hill in Rome

IV.

18   Nōbilibus, quī honōrēs et magistrātūs gerunt, necesse est facere
19 vestibula rēgālia et alta, ātria et peristȳlia magna, silvās et am-
20 bulātiōnēs longās. Praetereā bibliothēcās, basilicās magnificās, simi-
21 lēs basilicīs pūblicīs, facere dēbent, quod saepe et pūblica cōnsilia et
22 prīvāta iūdicia domī cōnficiunt.

Comprehension Questions

15. What five kinds of spaces do aristocrats who hold high office need
     in their homes? (18–20)
16. What else do these men need? (20–21)
17. What should the basilicas in their homes resemble? (20–21)
18. Why do they need these rooms in their homes? (21–22)

Interior of the Basilica Nova in the Roman forum

THE PASSAGE AS A WHOLE FOR DISCUSSION

I.

1   Nunc etiam necesse est animadvertere quōmodo in prīvātīs aedi-
2 ficiīs dēbeās aedificāre loca propria patribus familiārum et quōmodo
3 loca commūnia cum extrāneīs. Nam in haec quae propria patribus
4 familiārum sunt nēmō potest intrāre nisi invītātus, id est in cubicula,
5 trīclīnia, balneās, et cētera loca huius modī.

II.

6   Commūnia autem sunt ea loca, in quae hominēs dē populō, etiam
7 nōn invītātī, possunt venīre, id est vestibula, cavaedium, peristȳlia,
8 et cētera loca huius modī. Igitur eīs hominibus, quī commūnī
9 fortūnā sunt, nōn necessāria sunt magnifica vestibula nec tablīna
10 neque ātria, quod in aliīs officia praestant vīsitandō neque ab aliīs
11 vīsitantur.

III.

12   Hominēs quī frūctibus rūsticīs serviunt in vestibulīs stabula et
13 tabernās facere dēbent; in aedibus cryptās, horrea, apothēcās et
14 cētera quae frūctūs servent magis quam ēlegantiam addant. Item
15 faenerātōribus et pūblicānīs loca magna et pulchra et ab īnsidiīs tūta
16 conveniunt. Forēnsibus et ōrātōribus ēlegantia et spatiōsa loca con-
17 veniunt, in quibus conventōs excipere possunt.

IV.

18   Nōbilibus, quī honōrēs et magistrātūs gerunt, necesse est facere
19 vestibula rēgālia et alta, ātria et peristȳlia magna, silvās et am-
20 bulātiōnēs longās. Praetereā bibliothēcās, basilicās magnificās, simi-
21 lēs basilicīs pūblicīs, facere dēbent, quod saepe et pūblica cōnsilia et
22 prīvāta iūdicia domī cōnficiunt.

Discussion Questions

1. Vitruvius makes a distinction between rooms that are private and those that are public (1–8). From the plan of the **domus** given on page 3, find where the private rooms are placed and where the public rooms are placed. Why would this arrangement make sense?

2. What does Vitruvius mean by **commūnī fortūnā** (8–9)? Why do people in this situation need less space? What does this tell us about the uses of the **vestibula, tablīna,** and **ātria**?

3. How could you tell from the outside that a house belonged to someone who owned a working farm? (12–13) Is this different from or similar to the way farmers sell their produce today?

4. Why would money lenders and tax collectors need rooms that were roomy and nice, as well as safe? (14–16)

5. What kind of meetings do you think might take place in the houses of lawyers and public speakers? (16–17)

6. To the Romans, **nōbilis** meant political standing as well as social standing. What in Vitruvius' description of these men's houses tells us this? (18–22) Why did the **nōbilēs** need audience halls that were similar to public ones? (21–22)

2

THE *VIGILES*

Justinian, *Digest* I.15

(After Chapter 30)

INTRODUCTION

Before the time of Augustus there had been no official police force in Rome. The patron-client system (the system in which aristocrats protected their supporters from unfair treatment) had kept Rome running fairly smoothly for hundreds of years. However, from the time of the Gracchi brothers at the start of the second century B.C. and onward through a hundred years of civil strife, the social and political system at Rome declined. The social structure crumbled, and disorders broke out in the city. Crimes became an almost daily occurrence, with arson being one of the major problems.

Responding to this disruption of traditional Roman society, Augustus attempted to re-establish old values, unite the people, and bring peace and prosperity to the Roman world. As part of these efforts, he reorganized many aspects of urban life, and one matter that he attended to was the prevention of fires.

After a fire in 23 B.C., Augustus established a fire brigade of 600 slaves (**familia pūblica**) to be available when needed. Several more serious fires occurred, and Augustus established the fire brigade on a permanent basis, creating an official corps of 7,000 **vigilēs**. The **vigilēs** were equivalent to a combination of our policemen and firemen. They had various duties, one of which was to prevent and extinguish fires.

Very few Roman sources mention the **vigilēs**; the *Digest* of Justinian, however, contains a history of fire prevention in Rome and of the establishment of the **vigilēs** as well as a description of the duties of the **praefectus vigilum** (a combined police and fire chief in modern terms). Justinian was emperor from A.D. 527 to 565, and he appointed a commission of men to collect the works of those classical jurists who had written about the legal precedents affecting Roman public life. Paulus and Ulpianus were two of the writers whose works were included in the *Digest*. The passage from the *Digest* about the **vigilēs** includes extracts from both of these jurists. Hence some repetition will be seen in the following paragraphs.

1   **apud vetustiōrēs,** *among our ancestors*
      vetustiōrēs, literally, *the rather old ones*
      arceō, -ēre, -uī, *to prevent*
      triumvirī, -ōrum, m. pl., *board of three men* (responsible for supervising prisons
         and public safety)
      praesum, praeesse, praefuī, irreg. + dat., *to be in charge of*
         incendiīs arcendīs . . . praeerant, *were in charge of preventing fires*
      ab eō quod, *from the fact that*
2   **excubiae, -ārum,** f. pl., *nighttime guard duty*
      nocturnī, -ōrum, m. pl., *nightmen*
      dictī sunt, *were called*
3   **aedīlis, aedīlis,** gen. pl., **aedīlium,** m., *aedile* (public official in charge of streets,
         traffic, markets, and public games)
      tribūnus plēbis, tribūnī plēbis, m., *tribune of the plebs* (official responsible for
         protecting the rights of the plebs, the common citizens)
      familia pūblica, -ae, f., *gang of slaves under the control of the state*
      autem, conj., *moreover*
      circum, prep. + acc., *around*
4   **disposita erat,** *was placed/stationed*
      sī opus erat, *if there was need*
      ēvocō, -āre, -āvī, -ātus, *to call out, summon*
5   **prīvāta familia, -ae,** f., *gang of slaves under private control*
      mercēs, mercēdis, f., *wages, fee*
      grātīs, adv., *free, for nothing*

JUSTINIAN, *DIGEST* I.15

I.

1   Apud vetustiōrēs incendiīs arcendīs triumvirī praeerant, quī ab
2 eō quod excubiās agēbant nocturnī dictī sunt. Nōnnumquam et
3 aedīlēs et tribūnī plēbis adiūvērunt. Familia pūblica autem circum
4 portam et mūrōs disposita erat unde sī opus erat ēvocābātur. Fu-
5 erant et prīvātae familiae, quae incendia aut mercēde aut grātīs
6 exstinguerent.

Comprehension Questions

1. Who was in charge of preventing fires in olden days? (1)
2. What were they called and why? (1–2)
3. Who sometimes helped them? (2–3)
4. What additional help was available in emergencies? (3–6)

7 **dīvus, -a, -um,** *divine, deified*
8 **crēdō, crēdere, crēdidī, crēditus,** *to believe that* + acc. and infinitive
   rēs pūblica, reī pūblicae, f., *state, republic*
9 **salūs, salūtis,** f., *safety*
   melius, adv., *better*
   quam, adv., *than*
   cohors, cohortis, gen. pl., **cohortium,** f., *cohort* (a company of men brought together for a common purpose)
10 **opportūnus, -a, -um,** *suitable, convenient, strategic*
   locus, -ī, m., n. in pl., *place*
   cōnstituō, cōnstituere, cōnstituī, cōnstitūtus, *to station, post*
   quisque, quaeque, quidque, *each*
11 **tribūnus, -ī,** m., *officer, commander, supervisor*
   praeficiō, praeficere, praefēcī, praefectus, *to put someone* (acc.) *in charge of someone else* (dat.)
   spectābilis, -is, -e, *worthy of being looked at, notable, outstanding*
12 **praefectus, -ī,** m., *supervisor, deputy, commander*
   vigil, vigilis, m., *sentry, guard, member of the fire brigade*
   appellō, -āre, -āvī, -ātus, *to call, name*

13 **cognōscō, cognōscere, cognōvī, cognitus,** *to find out, learn, investigate, judge* (legal cases)
   incendiārius, -ī, m., *arsonist*
   effrāctor, effrāctōris, m., *housebreaker, burglar*
14 **fūr, fūris,** m., *thief*
   raptor, raptōris, m., *snatcher, robber*
   receptātor, receptātōris, m., *one who hides/shelters criminals*
   maximē, adv., *most, especially*
   atrōx, atrōcis, *terrible, cruel*
15 **fāmōsus, -a, -um,** *infamous*
   praefectus urbis, *urban prefect* (a magistrate who looked after public affairs for the emperor)
   plērumque, adv., *for the most part, in most instances*
16 **culpā** + gen., *by fault of, because of*
   fīunt, *happen*
   fūstis, fūstis, gen. pl., **fūstium,** m., *club, cudgel*
   castīgō, -āre, -āvī, -ātus, *to rebuke, punish*
17 **ignis, ignis,** gen. pl., **ignium,** m., *fire*
   vituperātiō, vituperātiōnis, f., *scolding*
   sevērus, -a, -um, *stern, harsh*

II.

7   Deinde dīvus Augustus ipse aliquid facere voluit quod fuerant
8 ūnō diē multa incendia. Crēdidit nēminem posse reī pūblicae
9 salūtem melius servāre quam sē ipsum. Itaque septem cohortēs in
10 opportūnīs locīs cōnstituit; quaeque cohors duās partēs urbis
11 custōdīvit. Tribūnōs eīs praefēcit et suprā omnēs spectābilem virum
12 quī praefectus vigilum appellātur.

Comprehension Questions

5. What made Augustus decide to do something? (7–8)
6. Why did he decide to take matters into his own hands? (8–9)
7. What were the three levels of the administrative structure that he
    established? (9–12)

III.

13   Cognōscit praefectus vigilum dē incendiāriīs, effrāctōribus,
14 fūribus, raptōribus, receptātōribus, sed virōs maximē atrōcēs et
15 fāmōsōs ad praefectum urbis mittit. Et quod plērumque incendia
16 culpā fīunt incolārum, aut fūstibus castīgat eōs quī neglegenter
17 ignem habent, aut vituperātiōne sevērā sine fūstibus.

Comprehension Questions

8. What is the difference between the type of criminals over whom
    the **praefectus vigilum** has jurisdiction and the type that is sent to
    the **praefectus urbis**? (13–15)
9. Who is chiefly to blame for fires? (15–17)
10. What two types of punishment can the **praefectus vigilum** inflict?
    (16–17)

18   **praefectus, -ī**, m., *supervisor, deputy, commander*
     vigil, vigilis, m., *sentry, guard, member of the fire brigade*
19   **calceātus, -a, -um**, *wearing sturdy shoes/boots*
     hama, -ae, f., *bucket, fireman's bucket*
     dolābra, -ae, f., *pickax*
20   **cūra, -ae**, f., *care*
     nē . . . fīat, *that . . . not break out*
21   **cēnāculum, -ī**, n., *top-story room, attic*

22   **īnsulārius, -ī**, m., *apartment dweller*
     ignis, ignis, gen. pl., **ignium**, m., *fire*
     apud sē, *among themselves, at home*
     potes: note the use of the second person in this paragraph of the *Digest*.
23   **fūstis, fūstis**, gen. pl., **fūstium**, m., *club, cudgel*
     flagellum, -ī, n., *whip*
     verberārī, *to be beaten*
     autem, conj., *moreover*
24   **praefectus urbis**, *urban prefect* (a magistrate who looked after public affairs for the
       emperor)

Model of a five-story **īnsula** at Ostia
Locate the **cēnācula.**

IV.

18 Praefectus vigilum per tōtam noctem vigilāre dēbet et per urbem
19 errāre calceātus cum hamīs et dolābrīs. Dēbet iubēre omnēs incolās
20 cūram habēre, nē neglegentiā incendium fīat. Praetereā omnēs in-
21 colās aquam parātam in cēnāculīs habēre iubet.

Comprehension Questions

11. What two things must the **praefectus vigilum** do? (18–19)
12. With what three things must he be equipped? (19)
13. What two things is he to order all the residents to do? (19–21)

V.

22 Īnsulāriōs quī neglegenter ignēs apud sē habeant potes iubēre
23 fūstibus aut flagellīs verberārī. Eōs autem, quī fūrtim incendium fa-
24 cient, ad praefectum urbis mittēs.

Comprehension Questions

14. How do the instructions given to the **praefectus vigilum** in lines
     22–23 differ from the description of the duties of the **praefectus
     vigilum** in lines 15–17?
15. Who should be sent to the **praefectus urbis**? (23–24)

THE PASSAGE AS A WHOLE FOR DISCUSSION

I.

1   Apud vetustiōrēs incendiīs arcendīs triumvirī praeerant, quī ab
2   eō quod excubiās agēbant noctūrnī dictī sunt. Nōnnumquam et
3   aedīlēs et tribūnī plēbis adiūvērunt. Familia pūblica autem circum
4   portam et mūrōs disposita erat unde sī opus erat ēvocābātur. Fu-
5   erant et prīvātae familiae, quae incendia aut mercēde aut grātīs
6   exstinguerent.

II.

7   Deinde dīvus Augustus ipse aliquid facere voluit quod fuerant
8   ūnō diē multa incendia. Crēdidit nēminem posse reī pūblicae
9   salūtem melius servāre quam sē ipsum. Itaque septem cohortēs in
10 opportūnīs locīs cōnstituit; quaeque cohors duās partēs urbis
11 custōdīvit. Tribūnōs eīs praefēcit et suprā omnēs spectābilem virum
12 quī praefectus vigilum appellātur.

III.

13 Cognōscit praefectus vigilum dē incendiāriīs, effrāctōribus,
14 fūribus, raptōribus, receptātōribus, sed virōs maximē atrōcēs et
15 fāmōsōs ad praefectum urbis mittit. Et quod plērumque incendia
16 culpā fīunt incolārum, aut fūstibus castīgat eōs quī neglegenter
17 ignem habent, aut vituperātiōne sevērā sine fūstibus.

IV.

18 Praefectus vigilum per tōtam noctem vigilāre dēbet et per urbem
19 errāre calceātus cum hamīs et dolābrīs. Dēbet iubēre omnēs incolās
20 cūram habēre, nē neglegentiā incendium fīat. Praetereā omnēs in-
21 colās aquam parātam in cēnāculīs habēre iubet.

V.

22 Īnsulāriōs quī neglegenter ignēs apud sē habeant potes iubēre
23 fūstibus aut flagellīs verberārī. Eōs autem, quī fūrtim incendium fa-
24 cient, ad praefectum urbis mittēs.

Discussion Questions

1. Who helped prevent and put out fires before Augustus organized the **vigilēs**? (1–6)
2. Does it appear that these arrangements were effective? What drawbacks might they have had? (1–6)
3. What attitude did Augustus have toward the situation? What does this reveal about his character and position? (7–12)
4. What social class do you suppose the men in the cohorts belonged to? Of what social class do you suppose the **tribūnī** and the **praefectus vigilum** were? (9–12)
5. What advantage can you see in the organizational structure that Augustus created? What does it tell us about the structure of Roman society? Who would be responsible to whom? How would the chain of command work? What powers would the **tribūnī** have? What power would the **praefectus** have? (9–12)
6. What are the responsibilities and legal authority of the **praefectus vigilum**? How might his powers be subject to abuse? (13–17)
7. With what is the **praefectus vigilum** equipped to deal immediately with emergencies? How effective could he be? (18–19)
8. What preventive measures does the **praefectus vigilum** take? How effective would they be? Why does he order water to be ready only in upper rooms? (19–21)
9. Do the punishments that the **praefectus vigilum** inflicts seem appropriate to the crimes? How do his powers differ from those of a modern policeman? (13–17 and 22–24)
10. To what extent do you think Augustus' measures were effective in achieving a better-organized and safer city?

3
THE *COMMISSATIO*

Seneca, *Moral Letters* LXXXIII.24–27

(After Chapter 34)

INTRODUCTION

The drinking party (**commissātiō**) was a popular after-dinner activity for the Romans. After the **cēna**, dinner guests would indulge in conversation and be entertained in various ways by their hosts, but they would often also indulge in heavy drinking. The **commissātiō** could easily become vulgar and distasteful. Guests would sometimes pass out, vomit, or become rude and obnoxious. Many Roman writers attribute the moral decline of Roman society and the abominable acts of some of its famous leaders to excessive drinking.

Seneca, a writer of the first century A.D., describes the aftermath of a **commissātiō** in his eighty-third *Moral Letter.* In this letter he illustrates how drinking ruined the once noble and illustrious Mark Antony, corrupting him and making him cruel.

Mark Antony was a Roman general. After Caesar's death he and Octavian fought against the tyrannicides Brutus and Cassius and their troops and defeated them, avenging the assassination of Caesar. They then divided the Roman Empire into two parts, with Octavian controlling the western part and Antony the eastern. Antony had married Octavian's sister, Octavia, to strengthen his alliance with Octavian, but in 37 B.C. he divorced her and married Cleopatra, the queen of Egypt. It was believed that Antony named Cleopatra the heir of the eastern provinces of the Roman Empire in his will. This rumor, the reign of terror that Antony instituted, and his order to have the head and hands of his enemy Cicero displayed publicly made him feared and detested by many Romans, even his own supporters. Octavian declared war on Antony and Cleopatra and in 31 B.C. defeated them at the battle of Actium.

Many writers believe that Antony's love for Cleopatra ruined him, but Seneca in this letter attributes his ruin to both love and wine. Seneca compares drinking to an illness that destroys a person's common sense and virtue. In keeping with his Stoic principles, Seneca recommends that all pleasures, such as drinking wine, be enjoyed in strict moderation.

1 **capere**, here, *to hold*
  palma, -ae, f., *palm* (leaf of the palm tree awarded to the victor in a contest)
2 **propīnātiō, propīnātiōnis**, f., *a drinking toast*
  vomitō, -āre, *to vomit continually*
3 **recūsō, -āre, -āvī, -ātus**, *to refuse*
  superstes, superstitis + dat., *surviving;* here as a substantive, *survivor*
  virtūs, virtūtis, f., *manliness, valor, perseverance*
4 **capāx, capācis** + gen., *able to hold much*
  dōlium, -ī, n., *large wine jug*

SENECA, *MORAL LETTERS* LXXXIII.24–27

I.

1   Quae glōria est capere multum? Cum palmam habueris et
2 propīnātiōnēs tuās convīvae somnō oppressī vomitantēsque
3 recūsāverint, cum superstes tōtī convīviō fueris, cum omnēs virtūte
4 magnificā vīceris et nēmō vīnī tam capāx fuerit, vincēris ā dōliō.

Comprehension Questions

1. To what activity does the opening question refer? (1)
2. What will the victor have? (1)
3. Why do the guests no longer respond to the toasts proposed by the victor in the drinking bout? (2–3)
4. To whom does the word **superstes** refer? (3)
5. How does the victor (**superstes**) compare with the others at the banquet? (3–4)
6. By what will the victor himself be overcome or surpassed? (4)

5　**M. = Marcus**
　nōbilis, -is, -e, *noble*
　quae alia rēs . . . quam, *what other thing . . . than. . . .*
　perdō, perdere, perdidī, perditus, *to destroy*
6　**externus, -a, -um,** *foreign, strange*
　mōs, mōris, m., *habit, custom;* pl., *character*
　vitium, -ī, n., *vice, fault*
　ēbrietās, ēbrietātis, f., *drunkenness*
7　**amor, amōris,** m., *love, desire*
8　**hostis, hostis,** gen. pl., **hostium,** m., *enemy*
　rēs pūblica, reī pūblicae, f., *state, commonwealth*
　impār, imparis, *ill-matched, not a match for*
　reddō, reddere, reddidī, redditus, *to give back, return; to render, make*
9　**crūdēlis, -is, -e,** *cruel*
　prīnceps, prīncipis, m., *emperor;* here, *leading citizen*
　cīvitās, cīvitātis, f., *state, commonwealth*
　cēnantī, *dining*
10　**rēgālis, -is, -e,** *royal*
　prōscrīptī, -ōrum, m. pl., *proscribed men.* This refers to Antony's political enemies, whose names were published on lists and who were then murdered with impunity. Their property was confiscated, and their heads and hands were brought to Antony. The famous orator Cicero was one such victim of Antony's proscriptions.
　ōs, ōris, n., *face, head*
11　**gravis, -is, -e,** *heavy;* here, *drunk*
　sitiō, -īre, -īvī, -ītus, *to thirst for, eagerly desire*

II.

5   M. Antōnium, magnum nōbilemque virum, quae alia rēs perdidit
6 et in externōs mōrēs ac vitia nōn Rōmāna addūxit quam ēbrietās et
7 Cleopatrae amor, quī nōn minor quam amor vīnī erat? Haec illum
8 rēs hostem reī pūblicae fēcit; haec hostibus suīs imparem reddidit;
9 haec crūdēlem fēcit. Nam capita prīncipum cīvitātis eī cēnantī allāta
10 sunt et inter convīvia magnifica et rēgālia prōscrīptōrum ōra ac
11 manūs agnōvit et vīnō gravis sitiēbat tamen sanguinem.

Comprehension Questions

7. How is Mark Antony initially described? (5)
8. What two things ruined him? (6–7)
9. Into what two things was he led? (6)
10. What three effects did all of this have on Mark Antony? (7–9)
11. What was brought to him while dining? (9–10)
12. In what circumstances did he identify the heads and hands of the proscribed? (10–11)
13. What did Mark Antony thirst for while drunk with wine? (11)

Marcus Antonius (Mark Antony) (ca. 82–30 B.C.)

12 **intolerābilis, -is, -e,** *intolerable*
    quod, *the fact that*
13 **ēbrietās, ēbrietātis,** f., *drunkenness*
    vīnolentia, -ae, f., *wine drinking*
14 **crūdēlitās, crūdēlitātis,** f., *cruelty*
    sequitur, *follows*
    corrumpō, corrumpere, corrūpī, corruptus, *to harm, disorder, ruin*
    ferōx, ferōcis, *fierce*
    morbus, -ī, m., *illness, disease*
15 **diūturnus, -a, -um,** *of long duration, chronic*
    difficilis, -is, -e, *difficult*
    continuus, -a, -um, *continuous*
16 **efferō, -āre, -āvī, -ātus,** *to make wild, savage* (**ferus, -a, -um**)
    apud sē, *in his right mind*
    īnsānia, -ae, f., *insanity*
17 **dūrō, -āre, -āvī, -ātus,** *to continue, last*
    vitium, -ī , n., *fault, vice*
    creō, -āre, -āvī, -ātus, *to create, cause*
    valeō, -ēre, -uī, -ītūrus, *to be strong*

18 **dēfōrmitās, dēfōrmitātis,** f., *ugliness, disgrace*
19 **verbum, -ī,** n., *word*
    Quod . . . est, *Which thing is. . . . , This thing is. . . .*
    probō, -āre, -āvī, -ātus, *to show, demonstrate*
        probā istās . . . poenās esse, *(just) show those things . . . to be. . . .*
    iste, ista, istud, *that;* pl., *those* (used contemptuously)
20 **voluptās, voluptātis,** f., *pleasure, delight*
    trānscendō, trānscendere, trānscendī, trānscēnsus, *to go beyond*
    modus, -ī, m., *limit*
    poena, -ae, f., *penalty, punishment*

III.

12   Intolerābile erat quod ēbrius fīēbat dum haec faciēbat; intolerābi-
13 lius erat quod haec in ipsā ēbrietāte faciēbat! Saepe vīnolentiam
14 crūdēlitās sequitur; animus enim corrumpitur et ferōx fit. Ut morbī
15 diūturnī hominēs īrātōs difficilēsque faciunt, ita ēbrietātēs continuae
16 efferant animōs. Nam ubi homō saepe apud sē nōn est, īnsānia
17 dūrat et vitia vīnō creāta etiam sine illō valent.

Comprehension Questions

14.   What was Mark Antony doing while identifying the heads and
      hands of the proscribed? (12)
15.   What was more intolerable than that? (12–13)
16.   What often follows wine drinking? (13–14)
17.   What two things happen to the mind of the wine drinker? (14)
18.   To what is continuous drunkenness compared? (14–15)
19.   What two things happen when a person is drunk often? (16–17)

IV.

18   Dīc igitur cūr vir prūdēns nōn dēbeat ēbrius fierī. Dēfōrmitātem
19 reī dēmōnstrā rēbus, nōn verbīs. Quod facillimum est, probā istās,
20 quae voluptātēs vocantur, ubi trānscendērunt modum, poenās esse.

Comprehension Questions

20.   What should sensible men not do? (18)
21.   What word does Seneca use to describe the state of drunkenness?
      (18–19)
22.   When do pleasures become punishments? (19–20)

THE PASSAGE AS A WHOLE FOR DISCUSSION

I.

1   Quae glōria est capere multum?   Cum palmam habueris et
2 propīnātiōnēs tuās convīvae somnō oppressī vomitantēsque
3 recūsāverint, cum superstes tōtī convīviō fueris, cum omnēs virtūte
4 magnificā vīceris et nēmō vīnī tam capāx fuerit, vincēris ā dōliō.

II.

5   M. Antōnium, magnum nōbilemque virum, quae alia rēs perdidit
6 et in externōs mōrēs ac vitia nōn Rōmāna addūxit quam ēbrietās et
7 Cleopatrae amor, quī nōn minor quam amor vīnī erat?   Haec illum
8 rēs hostem reī pūblicae fēcit; haec hostibus suīs imparem reddidit;
9 haec crūdēlem fēcit. Nam capita prīncipum cīvitātis eī cēnantī allāta
10 sunt et inter convīvia magnifica et rēgālia prōscrīptōrum ōra ac
11 manūs agnōvit et vīnō gravis sitiēbat tamen sanguinem.

III.

12   Intolerābile erat quod ēbrius fīēbat dum haec faciēbat; intolerābi-
13 lius erat quod haec in ipsā ēbrietāte faciēbat!   Saepe vīnolentiam
14 crūdēlitās sequitur; animus enim corrumpitur et ferōx fit. Ut morbī
15 diūturnī hominēs īrātōs difficilēsque faciunt, ita ēbrietātēs continuae
16 efferant animōs.   Nam ubi homō saepe apud sē nōn est, īnsānia
17 dūrat et vitia vīnō creāta etiam sine illō valent.

IV.

18   Dīc igitur cūr vir prūdēns nōn dēbeat ēbrius fierī. Dēfōrmitātem
19 reī dēmōnstrā rēbus, nōn verbīs. Quod facillimum est, probā istās,
20 quae voluptātēs vocantur, ubi trānscendērunt modum, poenās esse.

Discussion Questions

1. What similarities are there between the drinking bout as described in the first paragraph and military activity? Identify at least six words that are appropriate to both the drinking bout and military activity.

2. With what tone of voice would you read the opening question (1)? With what tone of voice would you read the words **virtūte magnificā** (3–4)? Does Seneca really want us to think that the victor in the drinking bout shows **virtūs magnifica**?

3. How is the wine jug personified? (4)

4. What charges does Seneca bring against Antony's drunkenness and his love of Cleopatra? (5–7)

5. What figure of speech does the position of the words **Haec . . . haec . . . haec** (7–9) illustrate? Why does Seneca employ it here? What effect does it have?

6. How does Antony's drinking affect his public life? (5–11)

7. How does it affect his personal behavior or character? (5–11)

8. In what ways does Seneca exaggerate or overdramatize in describing Antony's behavior? (5–11)

9. What difference is there between what was intolerable (**intolerābile erat**) in Antony's behavior and what was *more* intolerable (**intolerābilius erat**)? (12–13)

10. Examine the sentence **Saepe vīnolentiam crūdēlitās sequitur** (13–14). How does the order of the words in this sentence match the meaning?

11. How are the effects of chronic illness similar to those of continuous drunkenness? (14–16)

12. How does Seneca's final statement (19–20) illustrate the famous Greek maxim, "Nothing in excess" (= Latin **Nihil nimis**)? What does this maxim mean?

4

VIOLENCE IN THE STREETS OF ROME

Juvenal, *Satire* III.279–301

(After Chapter 35)

INTRODUCTION

This passage is a sketch by the poet Juvenal of someone being mugged in the streets of Rome. Juvenal was born in the town of Aquinum about 80 miles southeast of Rome. Little is known about his life: he came to live in Rome during the reign of the emperor Domitian, who ruled from A.D. 81 to 96, and he continued to live and write there under the next two emperors, Trajan and Hadrian.

Domitian became so strict about public morality toward the end of his reign that he had three of the Vestal Virgins executed for immoral conduct and the Chief Vestal buried alive. He also deprived the Senate of much of its influence; this policy, together with his criticism of the aristocracy's luxurious way of life, led to plots against him. These succeeded when he was murdered with the help of his own wife.

It is thought that something Juvenal wrote offended Domitian and that the writer was exiled to Egypt. Juvenal is supposed to have returned to Rome when the emperor was killed, feeling bitter about his exile. Under the more tolerant emperors Trajan and Hadrian, who followed Domitian, Juvenal published *Satires* (**Satūrae**) that have survived until today, but in these he writes only about the life and people of the past that he knew under Domitian, as though he were being careful not to make the same mistake twice.

In this passage from *Satire* III, Juvenal writes about life in the city of Rome. As you read this episode of someone being mugged, it is important to remember that Juvenal was a professional satirist writing just as a professional comedian would perform today. He was using techniques of rhetoric familiar to his readers. In this passage we can see his use of indignation (**indignātiō**), the deliberate appearance of justified anger to entertain, inform, or persuade. Since Rome was proud of its tradition of law-abiding citizens, the contrast between what happens in this scene and what ought to happen would be shocking if it were not recognized by the reader as an exaggeration for the sake of effect. Underneath the indignation, we can still sense the pride the Romans felt for their city and the values for which it was supposed to stand.

1 **petulāns, petulantis,** *aggressive*
   caedō, caedere, cecīdī, caesus, *to beat, kill*
   dat poenās, *pays the penalty, suffers punishment.* The phrase is ironic here.
2 **similis, -is, -e** + dat., *similar to, like*
   Achillēs, Achillis, m., *Achilles* (the great Greek warrior who fought at Troy and
      whose closest friend, Patroclus, was killed in battle, bringing Achilles great
      grief)
   lūgeō, lūgēre, lūxī, lūctus, *to lament*
3 **faciēs, -ēī,** f., *face*
   supīnus, -a, -um, *flat on the back*
   rixa, -ae, f., *brawl*

5 **quamvīs,** conj., *although*
   fervēns, ferventis, *boiling, seething*
   iuventās, iuventātis, f., *youth*
6 **obvius, -a, -um,** *who comes in his way, who meets him*
   coccinus, -a, -um, *scarlet*
   laena, -ae, f., *woolen cloak*
   comes, comitis, m./f., *companion*
7 **ōrdō, ōrdinis,** m., *line, row* (often used as a military term referring to lines of
      soldiers drawn up in their ranks)
   flamma, -ae, f., *flame, torch*
   aēneus, -a, -um, *bronze*
   lampas, lampadis, f., *lantern*
8 **lūna, -ae,** f., *moon*
   dēdūcō, dēdūcere, dēdūxī, dēductus, *to lead, bring, escort (home)*
   vel, conj., *or*
   candēla, -ae, f., *candle*
   fīlum, -ī, n., *wick*
9 **cautē,** adv., *carefully*
   cōnservō, -āre, -āvī, -ātus, *to protect, preserve*
   contemnō, contemnere, contempsī, contemptus, *to scorn, despise*

JUVENAL, *SATIRE* III.279–301

I. Domī

1   Vir ēbrius ac petulāns, quī nūllum hominem forte cecīdit, dat
2 poenās et tōtam per noctem iacet similis Achillī lūgentī amīcum
3 suum. Iacet in faciem, mox deinde supīnus. Modo rixa somnum
4 facit.

Comprehension Questions

  1. What kind of a man is being introduced in this passage? (1)
  2. What has he not done? (1)
  3. What is he now doing? (1–2)
  4. What is his present state of mind? (1–3)
  5. To whom is he compared? (2–3)
  6. What are the physical signs of the state of his mind? (3)
  7. What does this kind of person need in order to get to sleep? (3–4)

II. In Viā Rōmānā

5   Sed quamvīs malus atque fervēns iuventāte et vīnō, cavet et vītat
6 hominem obvium, quī coccinam laenam gerit et habet comitum
7 longissimum ōrdinem multāsque flammās et aēneam lampadem.
8 Mē, quem lūna solet dēdūcere vel brevis lūx candēlae, cuius fīlum
9 cautē cōnservō, contemnit.

Comprehension Questions

   8. How has the scene changed?
   9. How is our man now described? (5)
  10. What kind of man does he avoid if he encounters him in the
      streets? (5–7)
  11. What four things is such a man described as having? (6–7)
  12. What does the narrator have to guide himself home at night? (8)
  13. What does he carefully protect? (8–9)
  14. How does the bully regard him? (8–9)

10 cognōscō, cognōscere, cognōvī, cognitus, *to learn*
    initium, -ī, n., *beginning*
    rixa, -ae, f., *brawl*
    pulsō, -āre, -āvī, -ātus, *to beat*
11 vāpulō, -āre, -āvī, -ātus, *to be beaten, thrashed*
    contrā, adv., *in return; opposite, facing*
    stārī, *that (I) stop*
    pāreō, -ēre, -uī, -itūrus, *to obey*
12 quid agās, *what should you do?*
    cōgō, cōgere, coēgī, coāctus, *to force*
    furiōsus, -a, -um, *raving mad, frenzied*
13 tumeō, -ēre, -uī + abl., *to bulge with, be full of to the point of bursting*
    sūtor, sūtōris, m., *shoemaker*
    porrum, -ī, n., *leek* (a plant related to the onion)
    ēlixus, -a, -um, *boiled*
14 ovis, ovis, gen. pl., **ovium**, f., *sheep*
    comedō, comesse, comēdī, comēsus, *to eat* (*along with someone*)
15 calx, calcis, gen. pl., **calcium**, f., *heel* (used for kicking because the toes were
        unprotected), *a kick*
    cōnsistō, cōnsistere, cōnstitī, *to stop;* here, *to hang out*
16 tacitus, -a, -um, *silent, quiet*
    recēdō, recēdere, recessī, recessūrus, *to back off, withdraw*
    feriō, -īre, -īvī, -ītus, *to strike*
    pariter, adv., *equally, either way*
17 vadimōnia . . . faciunt, a legal term, *they make you give a security to appear in court*

18 lībertās, lībertātis, f., *freedom*
    pauper, pauperis, m., *poor man*
    pulsātus, -a, -um, *beaten, thrashed*
    pugnus, -ī, m., *fist*
    concīsus, -a, -um, *beaten, thrashed*
19 adōrō, -āre, -āvī, -ātus, *to beg*
    ut liceat . . . revertī, *that it may be permitted to return (home), that he may return
        (home)*
    dēns, dentis, gen. pl., **dentium**, m., *tooth*
    inde, adv., *from there*
    revertor, revertī, reversus sum, *to return*

III. Rixa

10   Cognōsce initium miserae rixae, sī rixa est, ubi tū pulsās, ego
11 vāpulō tantum. Stat contrā stārīque iubet. Pārēre necesse est, nam
12 quid agās, cum tē cōgat vir furiōsus et fortis? "Unde venīs?" exclā-
13 mat. "Cuius vīnō, cuius cibō tumēs? Quis sūtor porrum et ēlixam
14 ovis carnem tēcum comedit? Nīl mihi respondēs? Aut dīc aut accipe
15 calcem. Dīc ubi cōnsistās. In quā caupōnā tē quaerō?" Sī dīcere
16 temptēs aliquid aut tacitus recēdās, idem est. Tē feriunt pariter,
17 vadimōnia deinde īrātī faciunt.

Comprehension Questions

15. What happens now? (10)
16. How is this not a *real* brawl? (10–11)
17. What are the first two things the bully does? (11)
18. Why must the narrator obey? (11–12)
19. From where does the bully assume that the narrator is coming? (12–14)
20. What does the bully suggest the shoemaker served the narrator for dinner? (13–14)
21. Does the narrator answer the bully? (14)
22. What will happen if he remains silent? (14–15)
23. What are the bully's last requests? (15)
24. What difference does it make whether you reply or not? (15–16)
25. What two things do bullies do? (16–17)

IV. Lībertās Pauperis

18   Lībertās pauperis haec est: pulsātus rogat et pugnīs concīsus
19 adōrat ut liceat paucīs cum dentibus inde revertī.

Comprehension Questions

26. What is the narrator trying to define in these lines?
27. What has happened to the poor man? (18)
28. For what does he ask and beg? (19)

THE PASSAGE AS A WHOLE FOR DRAMATIC PERFORMANCE

This is an excellent passage for dramatic presentation. The following cast is needed:

Narrator
Bully
Rich man in scarlet cloak, followed by a string of attendants with
    torches and a bronze lamp
Speaker of the epilogue

The narrator steps forward, writes DOMI on the blackboard in large letters, and then reads lines 1–4 while pointing at the bully, who is lying on a mat on the floor, sleepless and tossing and turning.

The narrator then erases DOMI and writes IN VIA ROMANA on the board and draws a picture of a crescent moon in an upper corner of the board. He holds a candle in his hand. The bully has now risen from his mat and is looking about for trouble, flexing his muscles, grimacing, and stumbling as if drunk. As the rich man and his string of attendants approach from the back of the classroom, the narrator reads lines 5–9, pointing first to the bully and then to the rich man and his attendants, who approach the bully but pass him by without incident. While reading lines 8–9, the narrator points to himself, the crescent moon, and the candle that he is carrying.

The narrator then erases IN VIA ROMANA and writes RIXA on the board. The narrator begins reading the third paragraph by pointing to a burly student in the classroom and addressing the words of the first sentence to him. With the second sentence the narrator points to the bully on stage; the bully approaches and stands opposite the narrator. The third sentence is addressed to the audience, with a resigned shrug of the shoulders. Then the bully reads his lines in insulting, contemptuous, and threatening tones of voice, with appropriate mock actions, including kicking with his heel. The narrator has ignored the words of the bully and continues to ignore the bully as he (the narrator) reads lines 15–17 and addresses them to the audience, again shrugging his shoulders with resignation. As the narrator reads the last sentence of the paragraph, the bully does a pantomime of beating him and haling him off to court.

The bully continues his pantomime of beating the narrator, and the narrator gets down on his hands and knees and does a pantomime of pleading with the bully. The speaker of the epilogue now steps forward, erases RIXA from the board, and writes LIBERTAS PAUPERIS. He then reads lines 18–19, addressing them to the audience, while pointing at the narrator and the bully. When the speaker of the epilogue finishes, he erases LIBERTAS PAUPERIS and writes FINIS on the board.

I. Domī

1   Vir ēbrius ac petulāns, quī nūllum hominem forte cecīdit, dat
2 poenās et tōtam per noctem iacet similis Achillī lūgentī amīcum
3 suum. Iacet in faciem, mox deinde supīnus. Modo rixa somnum
4 facit.

II. In Viā Rōmānā

5   Sed quamvīs malus atque fervēns iuventāte et vīnō, cavet et vītat
6 hominem obvium, quī coccinam laenam gerit et habet comitum
7 longissimum ōrdinem multāsque flammās et aēneam lampadem.
8 Mē, quem lūna solet dēdūcere vel brevis lūx candēlae, cuius fīlum
9 cautē cōnservō, contemnit.

III. Rixa

10   Cognōsce initium miserae rixae, sī rixa est, ubi tū pulsās, ego
11 vāpulō tantum. Stat contrā stārīque iubet. Pārēre necesse est, nam
12 quid agās, cum tē cōgat vir furiōsus et fortis? "Unde venīs?" exclā-
13 mat. "Cuius vīnō, cuius cibō tumēs? Quis sūtor porrum et ēlixam
14 ovis carnem tēcum comedit? Nīl mihi respondēs? Aut dīc aut accipe
15 calcem. Dīc ubi cōnsistās. In quā caupōnā tē quaerō?" Sī dīcere
16 temptēs aliquid aut tacitus recēdās, idem est. Tē feriunt pariter,
17 vadimōnia deinde īrātī faciunt.

IV. Lībertās Pauperis

18   Lībertās pauperis haec est: pulsātus rogat et pugnīs concīsus
19 adōrat ut liceat paucīs cum dentibus inde revertī.

5
EARLY EDUCATION
IN ROME

Quintilian, *The Training of an Orator* I.3.8–13

(After Chapter 38)

INTRODUCTION

Rhetoric, the art of public speaking, comprised the third and final phase of a young Roman's education. This art was taught by rhetors, of whom one of the greatest was Marcus Fabius Quintilianus. He was born in A.D. 35 in what is modern Spain and was educated in Rome. As a young man, Quintilian went back home to teach but returned to Rome later in his career. He wrote a book, *The Training of an Orator*, on the course of study necessary to educate an orator. In this book Quintilian deals with every aspect of education from early youth to old age. Some sections deal specifically and extensively with the study of grammar. Other parts treat the attitudes necessary for teachers and students and other aspects of education. The following passage is from the first chapter, which discusses the education of the very young. It gives us a clear picture of Quintilian's concern for students, his understanding of teaching, and his good common sense.

School scene showing a pupil arriving late

1   **remissiō, remissiōnis**, f., *relaxation*
    nōn sōlum, *not only*
2   **quia**, conj., *because*
    continuus, -a, -um, *uninterrupted*
    perferō, perferre, pertulī, perlātus, irreg., *to endure*
3   **sēnsus, -ūs**, m., *sensation, feeling*
    anima, -ae, f., *soul; breath, life*
    careō, -ēre, -uī, -itūrus + abl., *to be without, lack*
4   **alternus, -a, -um**, *in alternation, in turn*
    retendō, retendere, retendī, retentus, *to relax, unbend* (e.g., a bow)
    sed quod, *but (also) because*
    discō, discere, didicī, *to learn*
    voluntās, voluntātis, f., *wish, will*
       suā voluntāte, *of their own will*
5   **cōgō, cōgere, coēgī, coāctus**, *to compel, force*
    renovātus, -a, -um, *renewed, refreshed*
    recēns, recentis, *untired, fresh*
    ad discendum, *to learning, to their studies*
6   **vīrēs, vīrium**, f. pl., *strength*
    ācer, ācris, ācre, *keen, sharp, acute*
    necessitās, necessitātis, f., *necessity, demands*
    nimius, -a, -um, *excessive*
7   **repugnō, -āre, -āvī, -ātūrus** + dat., *to fight against, rebel against*

QUINTILIAN, *THE TRAINING OF AN ORATOR* I.3.8–13

I.

1 Dēbēs omnibus discipulīs aliquam remissiōnem dare; nōn sōlum
2 quia nūlla rēs continuum labōrem perferre potest (atque ea quoque,
3 quae sēnsū et animā carent, servāre vim suam possunt modo sī
4 quiēte alternā retenduntur) sed quod puerī discunt suā voluntāte,
5 quae cōgī nōn potest. Itaque renovātī ac recentēs ad discendum af-
6 ferunt plūs vīrium et ācriōrem animum, quī necessitātī nimiī labōris
7 repugnat.

Comprehension Questions

1. What does Quintilian think all students should be given? (1)
2. What is the first reason that he gives for this? (2)
3. What do even inanimate things need if they are to retain their power? (2–4) What are some examples of things that need this?
4. What is the second reason that Quintilian gives? (4–5)
5. What do refreshed students bring to their studies? (5–6)
6. Against what does a sharper mind rebel? (6–7)

A Roman schoolboy

8 **offendō, offendere, offendī, offēnsus**, *to displease*
   lūsus, -ūs, m., *sport, game, play, playfulness*
   alacritās, alacritātis, m., *liveliness*
9 **dēmissus, -a, -um**, *downcast*
   studia, -ōrum, n. pl., *studies, learning*
   ācer, ācris, ācre, *keen, sharp, acute*
10 **mēns, mentis**, f., *mind*
   impetus, -ūs, m., *vigor, enthusiasm*
   nātūrālis, -is, -e, *proper to, appropriate to* + dat.
   aetās, aetātis, f., *age*
11 **modus, -ī**, m., *way, method, limit*
   remissiō, remissiōnis, f., *relaxation*
12 **odium, -ī**, n., *dislike, hatred*
   negō, -āre, -āvī, -ātus, *to deny, withhold*
   ōtium, -ī, n., *leisure, relaxation*
   cōnsuētūdō, cōnsuētūdinis, f., *custom, habit*
13 **nimius, -a, -um**, *excessive*
   acuō, acuere, acuī, acūtus, *to sharpen*
   ingenium, -ī, n., *intelligence, ingenuity*
14 **ubi (puerī)**, *when boys.* . . .
   invicem, adv., *in turn.* The adverb modifies **pōnentēs**.
   genus, generis, n., *kind*
      omnis generis, *of all kinds*
   quaestiuncula, -ae, f., *little questions*
   pōnentēs, nom. pl., modifying **puerī** (understood)
15 **aemulor, -ārī, -ātus sum**, *to compete*

Roman children at play

II.

8 Nec mē offendit lūsus in puerīs, nam est et hoc signum alacritātis.
9 Neque puer trīstis semperque dēmissus appropinquāre studiīs ācrī
10 cum mente potest, quod impetum nātūrālem aetātī illī nōn habet.
11 Necesse est tamen modum esse remissiōnibus. Ita nōn erit aut
12 odium studiōrum propter negātās remissiōnēs aut ōtiī cōnsuētūdō
13 propter nimiās. Sunt etiam multī lūsūs quibus acuere ingenium
14 puerōrum potes, ubi invicem omnis generis quaestiunculās pōnentēs
15 aemulantur.

Comprehension Questions

7. Why does Quintilian approve of playfulness in children? (8–10)
8. What reason does Quintilian give for why the student who is
    trīstis and **dēmissus** is not able to study well? (9–10)
9. What would result if relaxation were denied? (11–12)
10. What would result if there were too much relaxation? (12–13)
11. What purpose can play serve? (13–14)
12. What kind of game does Quintilian mention? (14–15)

Roman children at play

16   **mōrēs, mōrum**, m. pl., *character*
     lūsus, -ūs, m., *sport, play, playfulness*
     dētegō, dētegere, dētēxī, dētēctus, *to uncover, expose, reveal*
17   **aetās, aetātis**, f., *age, time of life*
     prāvus, -a, -um, *wrong*
     discō, discere, didicī, *to learn*
18   **fōrmō, -āre, -āvī, -ātus**, *to mold, fashion, train*
     cēdō, cēdere, cessī, cessūrus, *to come, go; to yield to* + dat.
19   **frangō, frangere, frēgī, frāctus**, *to break, crush*
     indūrēscō, indūrēscere, indūruī, *to harden, set, become firmly established*
          quae in prāvum indūruērunt, *that have hardened into wrongheadedness*
20   **corrigō, corrigere, corrēxī, corrēctus**, *to straighten out, set right*
     prōtinus, adv., *immediately, from the beginning*
     ergō, conj., *therefore*
     moneō, -ēre, -uī, -itus, *to advise, warn*
     nē . . . faciat (21), *that he not do, not to do*
     quid, *anything*
     cupidē, adv., *greedily*
21   **improbē**, adv., *shamelessly, dishonestly*
     impotenter, adv., *without self-control, wildly*
22   **Vergiliānus, -a, -um**, *of Vergil* (the great Roman epic poet)
          illud Vergiliānum, *that (famous saying) of Vergil.* The quotation comes from
               Vergil's book on farming, the *Georgics* II.272.
23   **Adeō . . . multum est**, *It is so important. . . .*
     in tenerīs, *in things of tender age*
     cōnsuēscō, cōnsuēscere, cōnsuēvī, cōnsuētus, *to become accustomed, form habits*

III.

16   Mōrēs quoque sē inter lūsūs facilius dētegunt. Nam etiam īnfirma
17 aetās rēctum prāvumque discere potest. Necesse est maximē puerōs
18 fōrmāre in illā aetāte quae simulāre nescit et magistrīs facillimē cēdit.
19 Facilius est enim frangere ea quae in prāvum indūruērunt quam
20 corrigere. Prōtinus ergō monēre puerum necesse est nē quid cupidē,
21 nē quid improbē, nē quid impotenter faciat. Dēbēs in animō semper
22 habēre illud Vergiliānum:

23   Adeō in tenerīs cōnsuēscere multum est.

Comprehension Questions

13. What reveals itself during games? (16)
14. What are children of even the youngest (**īnfirma**) age able to learn?
     (16–17)
15. For what two reasons is this age especially suitable for educating
     children? (17–18)
16. Why is it better not to wait until habits have "hardened into
     wrongheadedness"? (19–20)
17. What three things should children be warned against from the be-
     ginning? (20–21)
18. What, according to Vergil, is of great importance in the young?
     (23)

THE PASSAGE AS A WHOLE FOR DISCUSSION

I.

1   Dēbēs omnibus discipulīs aliquam remissiōnem dare; nōn sōlum
2 quia nūlla rēs continuum labōrem perferre potest (atque ea quoque,
3 quae sēnsū et animā carent, servāre vim suam possunt modo sī
4 quiēte alternā retenduntur) sed quod puerī discunt suā voluntāte,
5 quae cōgī nōn potest. Itaque renovātī ac recentēs ad discendum af-
6 ferunt plūs vīrium et ācriōrem animum, quī necessitātī nimiī labōris
7 repugnat.

II.

8   Nec mē offendit lūsus in puerīs, nam est et hoc signum alacritātis.
9 Neque puer trīstis semperque dēmissus appropinquāre studiīs ācrī
10 cum mente potest, quod impetum nātūrālem aetātī illī nōn habet.
11 Necesse est tamen modum esse remissiōnibus. Ita nōn erit aut
12 odium studiōrum propter negātās remissiōnēs aut ōtiī cōnsuētūdō
13 propter nimiās. Sunt etiam multī lūsūs quibus acuere ingenium
14 puerōrum potes, ubi invicem omnis generis quaestiunculās pōnentēs
15 aemulantur.

III.

16   Mōrēs quoque sē inter lūsūs facilius dētegunt. Nam etiam īnfirma
17 aetās rēctum prāvumque discere potest. Necesse est maximē puerōs
18 fōrmāre in illā aetāte quae simulāre nescit et magistrīs facillimē cēdit.
19 Facilius est enim frangere ea quae in prāvum indūruērunt quam
20 corrigere. Prōtinus ergō monēre puerum necesse est nē quid cupidē,
21 nē quid improbē, nē quid impotenter faciat. Dēbēs in animō semper
22 habēre illud Vergiliānum:

23   Adeō in tenerīs cōnsuēscere multum est.

Discussion Questions

1. To what extent does Quintilian support the need for relaxation? Why is relaxation necessary for students? How can relaxation be considered a part of education?

2. Why does Quintilian say there has to be a limit to relaxation? How does he balance relaxation with education? Do you agree with this argument? Why?

3. What example does Quintilian give of educational games? What examples can you give of educational games today? How do they affect learning? Are there games outside of the classroom in which you can learn things?

4. What reasons does Quintilian give for forming character at an early age? Why is it necessary to teach children right from wrong from the very beginning? Are these reasons still valid? When do you think children should learn right from wrong?

6
AN UNEXPECTED BATH
AT TRIMALCHIO'S

Petronius, *Satyricon* 72–73

(After Chapter 43)

INTRODUCTION

To the citizens of the Roman Empire, a bath was more than just a method for cleansing the body. It was a social ritual and an integral part of the day's routine. Romans would go to the baths to exercise, relax, or informally attend to important business. Socializing on a grand scale would be done at the large public **thermae**, but wealthy citizens might have their own **balneae** that were as refreshing but not as large as the public baths. These might be private clubs or smaller baths attached to urban villas of the upper class. Although smaller than the **thermae**, the **balneae** would still consist of three rooms: a hot room (**caldārium**), warm room (**tepidārium**), and cold room (**frīgidārium**). Vitruvius, a Roman architect, wrote that the location of the bath in a villa should "face away from the north and northeast" and that "the hot and tepid baths should be lighted from the southwest," thus taking advantage of solar energy. In Britain and other colder parts of the Empire, the hypocaust systems that heated the bath would double as the central heating for the entire villa. In the second century B.C., these household baths began to be constructed commonly in the homes of wealthy people and enabled them to avoid the more democratic **thermae**.

In the *Satyricon*, Petronius gives us a comic glimpse of how these private baths might have been utilized by the willing and the not-so-willing. His three anti-heroes, Encolpius (the narrator), his slave Giton, and his companion Ascyltos (note the Greek endings on the second and third names), accept an invitation to a dinner party given by Trimalchio, a freedman who has amassed an incredible fortune. During the lavish and lengthy affair, our friends are treated not only to displays of Trimalchio's fantastic wealth in the world of the living, but also to a glimpse of how he will show his riches and opulence after he dies. A detailed description of his tomb reduces himself and his guests to weeping and lamenting, and Trimalchio then suggests that a jump in his hot tub would cheer everyone up.

1 **quod**, conj., *because*
   Trimalchiō, Trimalchiōnis, m., *Trimalchio* (the rich host of the dinner party)
2 **coniciāmus nōs**, *let us throw ourselves*
   nōn paenitēbit, *it will not cause (you) regret, you won't be sorry*
3 **caleō, -ēre, -uī**, *to be hot*
   furnus, -ī, m., *oven*
4 **Habinnās, -ae**, m., *Habinnas* (one of the guests at the banquet; a Greek name—note
       the Greek ending of the nominative singular)
   nūdus, -a, -um, *bare*
   cōnsurgō, cōnsurgere, cōnsurrēxī, cōnsurrēctūrus, *to rise, get up*
5 **subsequor, subsequī, subsecūtus sum**, *to follow*

PETRONIUS, *SATYRICON* 72–73

I.

1 "Quod nōbīs morī necesse est," inquit Trimalchiō, "vīvere iam
2 dēbēmus. Coniciāmus nōs in balneās. Tum vidēbō vōs fēlīcēs et nōn
3 paenitēbit. Sīc calent balneae tamquam furnus." "Vērō, vērō," in-
4 quit Habinnās, "dē ūnā diē duās facere optimum est," nūdīsque cōn-
5 surrēxit pedibus et Trimalchiōnem gaudentem subsequī coepit.

Comprehension Questions

1. Why does Trimalchio propose that the guests go to his baths? (1–
    2)
2. How will bathing affect the guests? (2–3)
3. How hot are the baths? (3)
4. What reason does Habinnas give for approving Trimalchio's pro-
    posal? (3–4)
5. What sign of haste does Habinnas show as he follows Trimalchio
    to the baths? (4–5)

6   **respiciō, respicere, respexī, respectus,** *to look (at)*
    Ascyltos, -ī, m., *Ascyltos* (a companion of the narrator; a Greek name; note the Greek ending of the nominative singular; the accusative singular is **Ascylton**)

7   **expīrō, -āre, -āvī, -ātus,** *to breathe one's last, die*
    assentor, -ārī, -ātus sum, *to agree, go along with*
      assentēmur, *let us agree, let us go along* (with the proposal)

9   **Gītōn, Gītōnis,** m., *Giton* (the slave of the narrator)
    porticus, -ūs, f., *portico* (covered walk having its roof supported by columns)

10 **catēnārius, -a, -um,** *chained up, that is on a chain*

11 **pictus, -a, -um,** *painted* (on the wall). Ascyltos had seen a wall-painting of a dog guarding the doorway when the party had entered the house.

13 **ātriēnsis, ātriēnsis,** gen. pl., **ātriēnsium,** m., *slave in charge of looking after the household, steward*
    plācō, -āre, -āvī, -ātus, *to calm down, appease, placate*

14 **siccus, -a, -um,** *dry.* Here the adjective is being used as a substantive (*onto the dry pavement*).

15 **petō, petere, petiī** or **petīvī, petītus,** *to look for, seek; to beg*
    ut nōs . . . ēmitteret, *to let us go*

16 **putō, -āre, -āvī, -ātus,** *to think*
    hāc . . . quā, *this (way) by which, the same way*

Mosaic of a dog guarding the entrance to a house in Pompeii

II.

6   Ego respiciēns ad Ascylton, "Quid cōgitās?" inquam. "Ego enim
7 sī vīderō balneās, statim expīrābō." "Assentēmur," inquit ille, "et
8 dum illī balneās petunt, nōs in turbā exībimus." Cum haec placuis-
9 sent, Gītōn nōs per porticum dūxit et ad iānuam vēnimus, ubi canis
10 catēnārius nōs magnō tumultū excēpit et Ascyltos perterritus in pis-
11 cīnam cecidit. Ego quoque ēbrius, quī etiam pictum timueram
12 canem, dum natantī auxilium ferō, in eandem piscīnam tractus sum.
13 Servāvit nōs tamen ātriēnsis, quī et canem plācāvit et nōs trementēs
14 extrāxit in siccum.

Comprehension Questions

  6. How does the narrator feel about taking a bath? (6–7)
  7. What does Ascyltos propose that they do? (7–8)
  8. What happens when they reach the door? (9–11)
  9. What two reasons does the narrator suggest for why he was
     dragged into the pool? (11–12)
  10. What two reasons can you suggest for why the narrator and Ascyl-
     tos are **trementēs**? (13)

III.

15   Cum frīgidī petīssēmus ab ātriēnse ut nōs extrā iānuam ēmitteret,
16 "Errās," inquit, "sī putās tē exīre hāc posse quā vēnistī. Nēmō
17 umquam convīvārum per eandem iānuam ēmissus est; aliā intrant,
18 aliā exeunt."

Comprehension Questions

  11. What do the narrator and his friends beg of the steward? (15)
  12. In what are the narrator and his friends mistaken? (16)
  13. What is the rule about coming and going at Trimalchio's house?
     (16–18)

19 ātriēnsis, ātriēnsis, gen. pl., ātriēnsium, m., *slave in charge of looking after the house-*
       hold, steward
    ut . . . dūceret, *to lead*
    prōiciō, prōicere, prōiēcī, prōiectus, *to throw forth, fling*
20 siccō, -āre, -āvī, -ātus, *to dry*
    angustus, -a, -um, *narrow*
21 cisterna, -ae, f., *cistern* (an underground tank for storing water)
    frīgidārius, -a, -um, *for cold water*
    rēctus, -a, -um, *upright*
22 pūtidus, -a, -um, *rotting, foul, offensive*
    iactātiō, iactātiōnis, f., *boasting*
23 aliquandō, adv., *formerly*
24 pīstrīnum, -ī, n., *bakery*

IV.

19   Rogāvimus ātriēnsem ut nōs ad balneās dūceret, prōiectīsque
20   vestīmentīs, quae Gītōn siccāre coepit, balneās intrāvimus, angustās
21   et similēs cisternae frīgidāriae, in quibus Trimalchiō rēctus stābat.
22   Ac nē sīc quidem pūtidissimam eius iactātiōnem licuit effugere.
23   "Nihil," inquit, "melius est quam sine turbā lavārī. In hōc locō ali-
24   quandō pīstrīnum fuit." Deinde dēfessus cōnsēdit.

Comprehension Questions

14. What do the narrator and his friends now ask the steward? (19)
15. What job does Giton undertake? (20)
16. What two things are we told about the physical appearance of the
      baths? (20–21)
17. What does the narrator think about what Trimalchio says in the
      baths? (22)
18. What attitude does Trimalchio appear to have toward the crowds
      at the public baths? (23)
19. How has the place where Trimalchio is standing been improved
      from its earlier condition? (23–24)

25 **sonus, -ūs**, m., *sound*
   dīdūcō, dīdūcere, dīdūxī, dīductus, *to split, open up*
   usque ad + acc., *clear up to*
   camera, -ae, f., *vaulted ceiling*
26 **Menecratēs, Menecratis**, m., *Menecrates* (a famous Greek musician and composer
      of Nero's time)
   canticum, -ī, n., *song*
   lacerō, -āre, -āvī, -ātus, *to tear to pieces*
   sīcut, conj., *as*
27 **intellegō, intellegere, intellēxī, intellēctus**, *to understand*

28 **lābrum (= lavābrum), -ī**, n., *large basin for bathing*
   iungō, iungere, iūnxī, iūnctus, *to join*
29 **restringō, restringere, restrīnxī, restrictus**, *to tie or fasten behind one*
   ānulus, -ī, m., *ring*
   pavīmentum, -ī, n., *tiled floor*
30 **tollō, tollere, sustulī, sublātus**, *to lift, pick up*
   genū, -ūs, n., *knee*
   cervīx, cervīcis, f., *neck*
   post, prep. + acc., *after, behind*
   flectō, flectere, flexī, flexus, *to bend*
31 **tangō, tangere, tetigī, tāctus**, *to touch*

Frīgidārium of the Stabian Baths in Pompeii
Cēterī convīvae circum lābrum manibus iūnctīs currēbant.

V.

25   Invītātus balneārum sonō dīdūxit usque ad cameram ōs ēbrium
26 et coepit Menecratis cantica lacerāre, sīcut illī dīcēbant quī linguam
27 eius intellegēbant.

Comprehension Questions

20. What encourages Trimalchio to sing? (25)
21. In what unflattering way is his singing described? (26)
22. Why couldn't the narrator understand Trimalchio's song? (26–27)

VI.

28   Cēterī convīvae circum lābrum manibus iūnctīs currēbant et rīsū
29 ingentī clāmābant. Aliī autem restrictīs manibus ānulōs dē pavī-
30 mentō cōnābantur tollere aut positō genū cervīcēs post terga flectere
31 et pedēs tangere. Nōs, dum aliī sibi lūdōs faciunt, in aquam dē-
32 scendimus.

Comprehension Questions

23. Three groups of bathers are described. What is each group doing?
      (28–29, 29–30, and 30–31)
24. Do the narrator and his companions join in the games? (31–32)

THE PASSAGE AS A WHOLE FOR DISCUSSION

I.

1   "Quod nōbīs morī necesse est," inquit Trimalchiō, "vīvere iam
2   dēbēmus. Coniciāmus nōs in balneās. Tum vidēbō vōs fēlīcēs et nōn
3   paenitēbit. Sīc calent balneae tamquam furnus." "Vērō, vērō," in-
4   quit Habinnās, "dē ūnā diē duās facere optimum est," nūdīsque cōn-
5   surrēxit pedibus et Trimalchiōnem gaudentem subsequī coepit.

II.

6   Ego respiciēns ad Ascylton, "Quid cōgitās?" inquam. "Ego enim
7   sī vīderō balneās, statim expīrābō." "Assentēmur," inquit ille, "et
8   dum illī balneās petunt, nōs in turbā exībimus." Cum haec placuis-
9   sent, Gītōn nōs per porticum dūxit et ad iānuam vēnimus, ubi canis
10 catēnārius nōs magnō tumultū excēpit et Ascyltos perterritus in pis-
11 cīnam cecidit. Ego quoque ēbrius, quī etiam pictum timueram
12 canem, dum natantī auxilium ferō, in eandem piscīnam tractus sum.
13 Servāvit nōs tamen ātriēnsis, quī et canem plācāvit et nōs trementēs
14 extrāxit in siccum.

III.

15 Cum frīgidī petīssēmus ab ātriēnse ut nōs extrā iānuam ēmitteret,
16 "Errās," inquit, "sī putās tē exīre hāc posse quā vēnistī. Nēmō
17 umquam convīvārum per eandem iānuam ēmissus est; aliā intrant,
18 aliā exeunt."

IV.

19 Rogāvimus ātriēnsem ut nōs ad balneās dūceret, prōiectīsque
20 vestīmentīs, quae Gītōn siccāre coepit, balneās intrāvimus, angustās
21 et similēs cisternae frīgidāriae, in quibus Trimalchiō rēctus stābat.
22 Ac nē sīc quidem pūtidissimam eius iactātiōnem licuit effugere.
23 "Nihil," inquit, "melius est quam sine turbā lavārī. In hōc locō ali-
24 quandō pīstrīnum fuit." Deinde dēfessus cōnsēdit.

V.

25 Invītātus balneārum sonō dīdūxit usque ad cameram ōs ēbrium et
26 coepit Menecratis cantica lacerāre, sīcut illī dīcēbant quī linguam
27 eius intellegēbant.

VI.

28   Cēterī convīvae circum lābrum manibus iūnctīs currēbant et rīsū
29 ingentī clāmābant. Aliī autem restrictīs manibus ānulōs dē pavī-
30 mentō cōnābantur tollere aut positō genū cervīcēs post terga flectere
31 et pedēs tangere. Nōs, dum aliī sibi lūdōs faciunt, in aquam dē-
32 scendimus.

Discussion Questions

1. What is Trimalchio's attitude toward living? Do you agree with it?
    Is he someone you would like to know or accept a dinner
    invitation from?
2. What does Habinnas mean by **dē ūnā diē duās facere optimum
    est** (4)? Do you think his view of happiness is like Trimalchio's?
    Would either or both of the men agree with the philosophy of life
    contained in the saying **carpe diem**?
3. Why do you suppose Encolpius and Ascyltos were not eager to en-
    ter the baths with the other guests? (6–8) Why do you think they
    were so eager to escape from Trimalchio's house? What does the
    attitude of Encolpius and Ascyltos seem to be toward the class of
    people with whom they have been dining?
4. A dog chained at the entrance to a Roman house (9–10) was
    usually used to keep out unwanted strangers. Can you think of an
    example from the world of mythology of an animal being used to
    keep people *in* instead of *out*? How does this suggest that we
    might view Trimalchio's house?
5. What elements of the scene around the pool suggest slapstick com-
    edy? (8–14) This mode of comedy is still very common. Can you
    think of any examples?
6. Why do you suppose Trimalchio's household has rules about
    coming and going through particular doors? (16–18) Can you
    think of any places you have been to that have rules of this sort?
7. Why do you suppose that Petronius emphasizes that Trimalchio
    was standing upright in the bath? (21)
8. What do you think the narrator finds particularly disgusting about
    Trimalchio's bragging (**iactātiō**)? (22)
9. What attitude do you think the narrator has toward the three
    groups of people playing games in the baths? (28–31)
10. What do you think about bathing in the middle of a dinner party?
    Do we do anything like it?

A scene in the Colosseum at Rome, showing gladiators, a wild-
beast fight, and passages and chambers under the floor

7
ALYPIUS CATCHES GLADIATOR FEVER

Augustine, *Confessions* VI.8

(After Chapter 49)

INTRODUCTION

Aurelius Augustinus was born in North Africa in A.D. 354. He was the son of Patricius, a Roman citizen, and Monica, a devout Christian. Following in the footsteps of his father, he was educated according to traditional Roman standards and became a teacher of public speaking (a **rhētor**). He taught at Carthage, Rome, and then Milan. Meditative and religious in temperament, he joined an eastern religious sect while still a young man. Study of Plato and Greek philosophy made him renounce that sect, and under the influence both of his mother and of St. Ambrose, bishop of Milan, he was converted to Christianity in 387. He was ordained a priest in 391, and four years later he became the bishop of the North African town of Hippo, where he remained until his death in 430.

Augustine lived in troubled times as the Roman Empire crumbled to its end. Twenty years before his death Rome was sacked by the Visigoth Alaric, and nine years after his death Carthage was captured by Germanic tribes that had crossed the Rhine, swept through Gaul and Spain, and crossed into Africa. Augustine and his writings represent an island of order amidst this sea of turmoil. The purity of his Latin style recalls the great qualities of the Roman writers of the Golden Age of Latin literature.

Augustine's two best-known works are his *Confessions*, which record his life, notably his conversion to Christianity, up to the year 388, and his *The City of God*, in which he contrasts the eternal kingdom of heaven with the passing kingdom of the world. He is known as one of the great fathers of the Roman Catholic Church.

Alypius, the subject of the following story from the *Confessions*, was born in the same town as Augustine and was a student of his. In the *Confessions* he is the source and subject of several tales of mischief, and Augustine describes Alypius' love of chariot races, which parallels his attraction to the gladiatorial displays in this passage. He was duly delivered from both "vices," Augustine recounts, by his conversion to Christianity, and he was eventually ordained a priest.

1 **nōn sānē**, *certainly not*
2 **praecēdō, praecēdere, praecessī, praecessus**, *to go somewhere before someone else does, to precede in going.* Alypius had gone to Rome before Augustine.
  ut . . . disceret, *in order to learn*
  iūs, iūris, n., *law*
  incrēdibilis, -is, -e, *unbelievable*
  gladiātōrius, -a, -um, *gladiatorial*
3 **cum** + subjunctive, *although*
4 **dētestor, -ārī, -ātus sum**, *to curse, hate*
  condiscipulus, -ī, m., *fellow student*
5 **prandium, -ī**, n., *lunch*

6 **recūsō, -āre, -āvī, -ātus**, *to object, protest, refuse to accept*
  familiāris, -is, -e, *friendly*
  violentia, -ae, f., *force, violence*
8 **fūnestus, -a, -um**, *deadly, murderous*
10 **intendō, intendere, intendī, intentus**, *to direct* (the mind, eyes)
12 **forte**, adv., *by chance; perhaps*
  explōrō, -āre, -āvī, -ātus, *to test, try to find out*
  utrum, interrog. particle, *whether*
  efficiō, efficere, effēcī, effectus, *to bring (it) about.* That is, to live up to his boast (line 10)

AUGUSTINE, *CONFESSIONS* VI.8

I.

1   Alypius, nōn sānē relinquēns viam dēmōnstrātam sibi ā paren-
2 tibus, Rōmam praecesserat, ut iūs disceret. Ibi incrēdibilī gladiātōriī
3 spectāculī studiō incrēdibiliter arreptus est. Cum enim vītāret et
4 dētestārētur tālia, quibusdam eius amīcīs et condiscipulīs forte dē
5 prandiō redeuntibus occurrit.

Comprehension Questions

1. To what extent was Alypius following in his parents' footsteps? (1–2)
2. Why did he go to Rome? (2)
3. With what was he seized there? (2–3)
4. What was his attitude toward gladiatorial shows? (3–4)
5. Whom did he chance to meet and on what occasion? (4–5)

II.

6   Illī eum recūsantem vehementer et resistentem familiārī violentiā
7 dūxērunt in amphitheātrum diēbus lūdōrum crūdēlium et
8 fūnestōrum, haec dīcentem: "Sī corpus meum in locum illum
9 trahitis, num et animum et oculōs meōs in illa spectācula potestis
10 intendere? Aderō sed animus aberit, ac sīc et vōs et illa superābō."
11 Quibus audītīs, illī vehementius eum addūxērunt sēcum, id ipsum
12 forte explōrāre cupientēs, utrum posset efficere.

Comprehension Questions

6. What did Alypius' friends do to him? (6–7)
7. On what occasion? (7–8)
8. What were his feelings about what his friends were doing to him? (6)
9. What does Alypius claim that his friends will *not* be able to do? (9–10)
10. How does Alypius plan to overcome or outmaneuver his friends? (10)
11. Did Alypius' words restrain his friends or spur them on? (11)
12. What did his friends want to find out? (11–12)

13   sēdēs, sēdis, gen. pl., sēdium, f., *seat*
     locō, -āre, -āvī, -ātus, *to place*
     ferveō, fervēre, ferbuī, *to boil, seethe*
     immānis, -is, -e, *huge; brutal, savage*
14   quia, conj., *because*
15   auris, auris, gen. pl., aurium, f., *ear*
16   cāsus, -ūs, m., *fall*
         quōdam pugnae casū, *at a fall* (of a gladiator) *in a match*
17   pulsō, -āre, -āvī, -ātus, *to strike*
     cūriōsitās, cūriōsitātis, f., *curiosity*
     quidquid illud esset, *whatever it might be*
18   etiam vīsum, freely translated, *even having seen it*
     contemnō, contemnere, contempsī, contemptus, *to despise, disregard*

III.

13   Quō ubi advēnērunt et sēdibus locātī sunt, fervēbant omnia im-
14 mānissimīs voluptātibus. Ille oculōs clausit, quia in tanta mala ani-
15 mum suum prōcēdere nōlēbat. Dēbuit etiam aurēs claudere! Nam
16 quōdam pugnae cāsū, cum clāmor ingēns tōtīus populī vehementer
17 eum pulsāvisset, cūriōsitāte victus et parātus, quidquid illud esset,
18 etiam vīsum contemnere et vincere, oculōs aperuit.

Comprehension Questions

13. In what state were the people in the amphitheater when Alypius
     and his friends arrived and were seated? (13–14)
14. Why did Alypius shut his eyes? (14–15)
15. What should he also have closed? (15)
16. What caused the people in the amphitheater to shout? (15–16)
17. With what was Alypius overcome? (17)
18. What was he ready to do? (17–18)

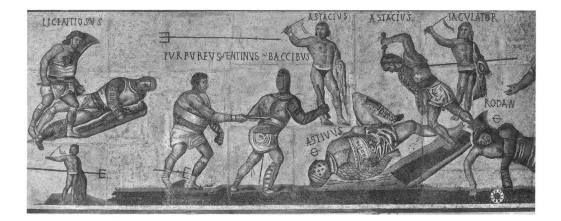

Gladiators on a Roman mosaic

22   āvertō, āvertere, āvertī, āversus, *to turn away*
23   hauriō, haurīre, hausī, haustus, *to draw* (water); *to drink, swallow*
     furiae, -ārum, f. pl., *madness, frenzy, desire, lust*
     certāmen, certāminis, n., *contest*
24   sangineus, -a, -um, *bloodstained, bloody*
     inēbriō, -āre, -āvī, -ātus, *to make drunk, intoxicate*
25   socius, -ī, m., *comrade, companion*

27   Quid plūra? *What more (should I say)?*
     exārdēscō, exārdēscere, exārsī, *to catch fire, burst into flame*
     īnsānia, -ae, f., *madness*
29   prae, prep. + abl., *before*

IV.

19   Statim percussus est graviōre vulnere in animā quam in corpore
20 ille gladiātor, quem vidēre cupīvit, ceciditque miserābilius quam ille,
21 quō cadente factus est clāmor. Ut enim vīdit illum sanguinem,
22 crūdēlitātem simul bibit. Nōn sē āvertit, sed dīligenter spectāvit.
23 Hauriēbat furiās et nesciēbat, et dēlectābātur scelere certāminis, et
24 sanguineā voluptāte inēbriābātur. Nec erat iam ille, quī vēnerat, sed
25 ūnus dē turbā, ad quam vēnerat, et vērus eōrum socius, ā quibus ad-
26 ductus erat.

Comprehension Questions

19. With what was Alypius struck? (19–20)
20. How is Alypius said to have suffered more than the gladiator? (19–21)
21. What did Alypius do when he saw the blood of the fallen gladiator? (21–22)
22. What was he not able to do? (22)
23. In what ways was his condition similar to that of a drunkard? (22–24)
24. How was he transformed into a different person from the person he had been when he arrived at the amphitheater? (24–26)

V.

27   Quid plūra? Spectāvit, clāmāvit, exārsit, abstulit inde sēcum īn-
28 sāniam, quā excitābātur redīre, nōn tantum cum illīs, ā quibus ad-
29 ductus erat, sed etiam prae illīs et aliōs trahēns.

Comprehension Questions

25. What did Alypius carry away from the amphitheater with him? (27–28)
26. What did he do after this visit to the amphitheater that he had not done before? (28–29)

THE PASSAGE AS A WHOLE FOR DISCUSSION

I.

1   Alypius, nōn sānē relinquēns viam dēmōnstrātam sibi ā paren-
2 tibus, Rōmam praecesserat, ut iūs disceret. Ibi incrēdibilī gladiātoriī
3 spectāculī studiō incrēdibiliter arreptus est. Cum enim vītāret et
4 dētestārētur tālia, quibusdam eius amīcīs et condiscipulīs forte dē
5 prandiō redeuntibus occurrit.

II.

6   Illī eum recūsantem vehementer et resistentem familiārī violentiā
7 dūxērunt in amphitheātrum diēbus lūdōrum crūdēlium et
8 fūnestōrum, haec dīcentem: "Sī corpus meum in locum illum
9 trahitis, num et animum et oculōs meōs in illa spectācula potestis
10 intendere? Aderō sed animus aberit, ac sīc et vōs et illa superābō."
11 Quibus audītīs, illī vehementius eum addūxērunt sēcum, id ipsum
12 forte explōrāre cupientēs, utrum posset efficere.

III.

13   Quō ubi advēnērunt et sēdibus locātī sunt, fervēbant omnia im-
14 mānissimīs voluptātibus. Ille oculōs clausit, quia in tanta mala ani-
15 mum suum prōcēdere nōlēbat. Dēbuit etiam aurēs claudere! Nam
16 quōdam pugnae cāsū, cum clāmor ingēns tōtīus populī vehementer
17 eum pulsāvisset, cūriōsitāte victus et parātus, quidquid illud esset,
18 etiam vīsum contemnere et vincere, oculōs aperuit.

IV.

19   Statim percussus est graviōre vulnere in animā quam in corpore
20 ille gladiātor, quem vidēre cupīvit, ceciditque miserābilius quam ille,
21 quō cadente factus est clāmor. Ut enim vīdit illum sanguinem,
22 crūdēlitātem simul bibit. Nōn sē āvertit, sed dīligenter spectāvit.
23 Hauriēbat furiās et nesciēbat, et dēlectābātur scelere certāminis, et
24 sanguineā voluptāte inēbriābātur. Nec erat iam ille, quī vēnerat, sed
25 ūnus dē turbā, ad quam vēnerat, et vērus eōrum socius, ā quibus ad-
26 ductus erat.

V.

27   Quid plūra? Spectāvit, clāmāvit, exārsit, abstulit inde sēcum īn-
28 sāniam, quā excitābātur redīre, nōn tantum cum illīs, ā quibus ad-
29 ductus erat, sed etiam prae illīs et aliōs trahēns.

Discussion Questions

1. How does Augustine refer to the gladiatorial games in Rome? What specific words in the Latin text convey his impressions of the spectacles? Is this attitude consistent with other attitudes toward the games that you have seen? Is this the attitude that most Romans would take? What do you think would account for Augustine's view of the games?

2. Examine lines 11–12, **Quibus audītīs . . . efficere**, carefully again. What do you think accounts for the desire of Alypius' friends to test his moral resolve? Can you think of other situations where friends act like this?

3. What was it that caused Alypius' downfall? Try to find a Latin word or phrase from the text that sums it up. Why do you think Alypius decided to open his eyes? (15–18)

4. Compare Alypius' initial attitude toward the games and what he says to his friends about them with his attitude and actions after he begins to watch them. What do you think accounts for this change in his attitude? Does one of his two personalities represent the "real Alypius"? If so, how do you explain the other personality, and why does Alypius present it?

5. Examine the terminology Augustine uses in lines 21–24, especially the verbs **bibit, hauriēbat, dēlectābātur,** and **inēbriābātur**. Why is the image of a drunkard especially appropriate in this passage?

6. Augustine describes, in an earlier episode in this book, how Alypius used to be wild about chariot races in a similar manner when he was living at Carthage. Is there any connection between Alypius' two "vices"? Can you think of any modern comparisons?

8

THE WEDDING
OF CATO AND MARCIA

Lucan, *Civil War* II.350–373

(After Chapter 53)

INTRODUCTION

While the Emperor Nero was in power at Rome (A.D. 54–68), the celebrations and ceremonies of Roman tradition reached excessive proportions. Many Roman poets and historians wrote, sometimes with admiration and sometimes with disgust, of Nero's extreme self-indulgence and of the decadence that it brought to Roman institutions. Some of these writers, in particular Seneca and Lucan, who were close to the emperor, reacted to Nero's excesses by holding up an ideal of behavior exactly the opposite of his. They praised restraint and strict moral discipline. Both Seneca and Lucan looked back to the time of the civil war between Julius Caesar and the Roman Senate and chose the Roman senator Cato as the model of ideal behavior. In his *Civil War*, Lucan praised not only Cato's commitment to the political institutions of the Roman Republic (510–31 B.C.) and his commitment to its traditions of liberty and freedom, all of which Cato had upheld on the side of the Senate against Caesar, but also his rejection of luxury and ostentation.

In the following passage Lucan describes Cato's wedding. As the civil war is beginning, Cato is approached by Marcia. Marcia and Cato had been divorced because Cato wanted her to marry someone else so that she could bear children. Now Marcia's recent husband has just died, and she wants to remarry Cato and share in his troubles. The wedding is unusual in many ways, not only because it is a remarriage during wartime, but also because of its excessive simplicity. Not only are luxury and display rejected, but so are even the simple festivities of customary weddings. This wedding is also unusual in that it is accompanied by elements of funeral rituals. The sterile marriage-that-is-no-marriage symbolizes the death of the old Republican values and form of government that Cato was fighting for. Eventually he commited suicide when he saw that with Caesar's victory the old values were lost forever.

It will be interesting to see how much we can learn about traditional weddings from this very unusual one.

1 **aliēnus, -a, -um** + dat., *inappropriate (for)*
2 **nūptiae, -ārum**, f., *marriage, wedding*
  fātum, -ī, n., *fate*
  foedus, foederis, n., *formal agreement, treaty, compact;* here, *marriage vows*
  iūs, iūris, n., *law;* here pl., *marriage ties, bonds*
3 **vānus, -a, -um**, *empty, hollow, meaningless*
  pompa, -ae, f., *funeral procession;* here, *ceremony, festivity*
  sacra, -ōrum, n. pl., *sacrifice;* here, *marriage rites*
  admittō, admittere, admīsī, admissus, *to commit* (a crime); here, *to admit, allow . . .*
    to come to + dat.
  testis, testis, gen. pl., **testium**, m., *witness.* Here translate *as witnesses.*
  pendeō, pendēre, pependī, *to hang, be suspended*
4 **fēstus, -a, -um**, *festive* (appropriate to special occasions that honor the gods)
  serta, -ōrum, n. pl., *garlands*
  corōnātus, -a, -um, *decked with garlands, wreathed*

Fēsta serta

LUCAN, *CIVIL WAR* II.350–373

I.

1   Marciae verba Catōnī persuāsērunt. Quamquam tempora sint ali-
2 ēna nūptiīs, iam fātō in bella vocante, tamen foedera sōla iūraque
3 sine vānā pompā placent sacrīsque deōs admittere testēs. Nōn pen-
4 dent fēsta serta in līmine corōnātō.

Comprehension Questions

1. What did Marcia succeed in doing? (1)
2. Why are the times not right for marriage? (1–2)
3. What three things do Cato and Marcia want? (2–3)
4. What do they not want? (3)
5. What is missing from the doorway? (3–4)

A Roman bride and bridegroom joining hands in marriage

5 **discurrō, discurrere, discurrī, discursūrus,** *to run this way and that*
   īnfula, -ae, f., *woolen headband* (knotted at intervals with ribbons and hung in
        doorways to mark religious ceremonies)
   geminus, -a, -um, *twin*
6 **lēgitimus, -a, -um,** *prescribed by law or custom, proper, customary*
   torus, -ī, m., *couch, marriage bed*
   gradus, -ūs, m., *step, pace;* pl., *stepped platform* (on which the marriage bed is
        placed)
   eburnus, -a, -um, *made of ivory*
   acclīnis, -is, -e + dat., *leaning on, resting on*
7 **vestis, vestis,** gen. pl., **vestium,** f., *clothing;* pl., *coverlet*
   pictus, -a, -um, *decorated*
   premō, premere, pressī, pressus, *to press, rest upon, weigh down*
   turrītus, -a, -um, *fortified/decorated with towers*
8 **contingō, contingere, contigī, contāctus,** *to touch*
   trānsferō, trānsferre, trānstulī, trānslātus, irreg., *to carry across*

9 **lūteus, -a, -um,** *yellow, reddish-yellow*
   leviter, adv., *lightly*
   tegō, tegere, tēxī, tēctus, *to cover*
   pudor, pudōris, m., *modesty, blush*
10 **vēlō, -āre, -āvī, -ātus,** *to cover*
   balteus, -ī, m., *belt, girdle*
   amictus, -ūs, m., *dress*
   fluxus, -a, -um, *flowing*
   gemma, -ae, f., *jewel, gem*
   astringō, astringere, astrīnxī, astrictus, *to tie, bind, hold in place*
11 **monīle, monīlis,** gen. pl. **monīlium,** n., *necklace*
   decēns, decentis, *fitting, pleasing, graceful*
   collum, -ī, n., *neck* (Latin often uses the plural of this word for a single neck)
   cingō, cingere, cīnxī, cīnctus, *to encircle*
   angustus, -a, -um, *narrow*
   suppara, -ōrum, n. pl., *scarf*
12 **nūdātus, -a, -um,** *bare*
   lacertus, -ī, m., *upper arm*
   umerus, -ī, m., *shoulder*
        umerīs prīmīs, *the upper part of her shoulders*

II.

5   Nōn discurrit īnfula alba in geminōs postēs. Nōn sunt taedae
6 lēgitimae. Nōn stat torus gradibus eburnīs acclīnis nec ostendit
7 vestēs pictās aurō. Nōn premit mātrōnae frontem corōna turrīta;
8 nōn vītat mātrōna contingere līmina pedem trānsferēns.

Comprehension Questions

6. What five things that are normal at a wedding are absent from this
ceremony? (5–7)
7. What does Marcia not avoid that a bride normally would? (8)

Corōna turrīta

III.

9   Nōn lūtea flammea leviter tēctūra timidum pudōrem nūptae
10 vēlāvērunt dēmissōs vultūs. Nec balteus amictūs fluxōs gemmīs as-
11 trīnxit. Monīle decēns colla nōn cingit, nec angusta suppara cingunt
12 nūdātōs lacertōs, haerentia umerīs prīmīs.

Comprehension Questions

8. What would the **lūtea flammea** normally worn by the bride do?
(9–10)
9. With what would the bride's belt often be decorated? What purpose did the belt normally serve? (10–11)
10. What would normally encircle the bride's neck? (11)
11. What would the bride's **suppara** normally cover? (11–12)

13   **sīcut,** conj., *just as*
    lūgubria, lūgubrium, n. pl., *mourning garments*
    maestus, -a, -um, *sad, mournful, appropriate to mourning*
    cultus, -ūs, m., *dress, appearance*
    quōmodo . . . hōc, *in the way . . . in this way*
14   **nātus, -ī,** m., *son*
    purpura, -ae, f., *purple border* (on Cato's tunic)
    tēctus, -a, -um, *covered*
    fūnereus, -a, -um, *funereal, worn at funerals*
15   **solitus, -a, -um,** *usual, customary*
    sāl, salis, m., *salt, wit;* pl., *jokes*
    Sabīnus, -a, -um, *Sabine.* The joking and jesting that accompanied weddings were
        thought to have originated with the Sabines, a people living to the northeast of
        Rome.
    convīcium, -ī, n., *abusive language, insults*
    fēstus, -a, -um, *festive* (appropriate to special occasions that honor the gods); here,
        playful
16   **excipiō, excipere, excēpī, exceptus,** *to welcome, receive*

17   **coeō, coīre, coiī, coitus,** irreg., *to come together*
    tacitus, -a, -um, *silent*
    contentus, -a, -um, *content, satisfied with*
18   **Brūtus, -ī,** m., *Marcus Junius Brutus* (one of the assassins of Julius Caesar)
    sānctus, -a, -um, *holy, sacred;* here, *upright, virtuous*
    capillī, -ōrum, m. pl., *hair*
    horrificus, -a, -um, *rough, unkempt*
    dīmoveō, dīmovēre, dīmōvī, dīmōtus, *to remove*
19   **dūrus, -a, -um,** *hard, harsh, severe*
    admittō, admittere, admīsī, admissus, *to commit* (a crime); here, *to admit, allow*

IV.

13   Sīcut Marcia erat, lūgubria maestī cultūs servat. Quōmodo am-
14 plexa est nātōs, hōc marītum. Purpura tēcta fūnereā lānā cēlātur.
15 Nōn erant solitī salēs. Nec mōre Sabīnō trīstis marītus convīcia fēsta
16 excēpit.

Comprehension Questions

12. In what was Marcia still clothed? (13)
13. How did Marcia embrace her husband? (13–14)
14. With what was the purple band of Cato's tunic covered and con-
      cealed? (14)
15. What did the husband not receive that was customary at wed-
      dings? (15–16)

V.

17   Familia nōn coiit, neque propinquī. Iunguntur tacitī contentīque
18 auspice Brūtō. Catō nec ab ōre sānctō capillōs horrificōs dīmōvit nec
19 dūrō in vultū gaudia admīsit.

Comprehension Questions

16. What people are absent from the wedding who would be expected
      to be present? (17)
17. What role does Brutus play at the wedding? (17–18)
18. How does Cato at the wedding express his sorrow over the
      calamities that his country was suffering in the civil war? (18–19)

THE PASSAGE AS A WHOLE FOR DISCUSSION

I.

1   Marciae verba Catōnī persuāsērunt. Quamquam tempora sint ali-
2 ēna nūptiīs, iam fātō in bella vocante, tamen foedera sōla iūraque
3 sine vānā pompā placent sacrīsque deōs admittere testēs. Nōn pen-
4 dent fēsta serta in līmine corōnātō.

II.

5   Nōn discurrit īnfula alba in geminōs postēs. Nōn sunt taedae
6 lēgitimae. Nōn stat torus gradibus eburnīs acclīnis nec ostendit
7 vestēs pictās aurō. Nōn premit mātrōnae frontem corōna turrita;
8 nōn vītat mātrōna contingere līmina pedem trānsferēns.

III.

9   Nōn lūtea flammea leviter tēctūra timidum pudōrem nūptae
10 vēlāvērunt dēmissōs vultūs. Nec balteus amictūs fluxōs gemmīs as-
11 trīnxit. Monīle decēns colla nōn cingit, nec angusta suppara cingunt
12 nūdātōs lacertōs, haerentia umerīs prīmīs.

IV.

13   Sīcut Marcia erat, lūgubria maestī cultūs servat. Quōmodo am-
14 plexa est nātōs, hōc marītum. Purpura tēcta fūnereā lānā cēlātur.
15 Nōn erant solitī salēs. Nec mōre Sabīnō trīstis marītus convīcia fēsta
16 excēpit.

V.

17   Familia nōn coiit, neque propinquī. Iunguntur tacitī contentīque
18 auspice Brūtō. Catō nec ab ōre sānctō capillōs horrificōs dīmōvit nec
19 dūrō in vultū gaudia admīsit.

Topics for Discussion

1. In what ways is the wedding that is described here an appropriate
    expression of Cato and Marcia's sorrow over the death of the Repub-
    lic in the Civil War?
2. Using the details of the description of the wedding of Cato and Mar-
    cia as a guide, describe a normal Roman wedding.

VOCABULARY

A

ā or **ab**, prep. + abl., *from, away from, by*

abstulī, see **auferō**

absum, abesse, āfuī, āfutūrus, irreg., *to be away, be absent, be distant*

ac, conj., *and*

accipiō, accipere, accēpī, acceptus, *to accept, get, receive, welcome*

ad, prep. + acc., *to, toward, at, near*

addō, addere, addidī, additus, *to add*

addūcō, addūcere, addūxī, adductus, *to lead on, bring*

adiuvō, adiuvāre, adiūvī, adiūtus, *to help*

adsum, adesse, adfuī, adfutūrus, irreg., *to be present, be near*

adveniō, advenīre, advēnī, adventūrus, *to reach, arrive (at)*

aedificium, -ī, n., *building*

aedificō, -āre, -āvī, -ātus, *to build*

afferō, afferre, attulī, allātus, irreg., *to bring, bring to, bring in*

agnōscō, agnōscere, agnōvī, agnitus, *to recognize*

agō, agere, ēgī, āctus, *to do, drive; to discuss, debate*

albus, -a, -um, *white*

aliquī, aliqua, aliquod, *some (or other)*

aliquis, aliquid, *someone, something*

alius, alia, aliud, *another, other, one . . . another*

        aliī . . . aliī . . ., *some . . . others . . .*

amīcus, -ī, m., *friend*

amphitheātrum, -ī, n., *amphitheater*

amplector, amplectī, amplexus sum, *to embrace*

anima, -ae, f., *soul*

animus, -ī, m., *mind, spirit, will*

aperiō, aperīre, aperuī, apertus, *to open*

appropinquō, -āre, -āvī, -ātūrus + dat. or **ad** + acc., *to approach, come near (to)*

aqua, -ae, f., *water*

arripiō, arripere, arripuī, arreptus, *to grab hold of, snatch, seize*

atque, conj., *and, also*

ātrium, -ī, n., *atrium, main room*

audiō, -īre, -īvī, -ītus, *to hear, listen to*

auferō, auferre, abstulī, ablātus, irreg., *to carry away, take away*

aurum, -ī, n., *gold*

auspex, auspicis, m., *augur, officiating priest*

aut, conj., *or*

    aut . . . aut, conj., *either . . . or*

autem, conj., *however, but, moreover*

auxilium, -ī, n., *help*

B

balneae, -ārum, f. pl., *baths*

bellum, -ī, n., *war*

bibō, bibere, bibī, *to drink*

brevis, -is, -e, *short*

C

cadō, cadere, cecidī, cāsūrus, *to fall*

canis, canis, m./f., *dog*

caput, capitis, n., *head*

carō, carnis, gen. pl., f., *meat, flesh*

caupōna, -ae, f., *inn*

caveō, cavēre, cāvī, cautus, *to be careful, watch out for, beware*

cēlō, -āre, -āvī, -ātus, *to hide, conceal*

cēterī, -ae, -a, *the rest, the others, other*

cibus, -ī, m., *food*

circum, prep. + acc., *around*

clāmō, -āre, -āvī, -ātūrus, *to shout*

clāmor, -ōris, m., *shout, shouting*

claudō, claudere, clausī, clausus, *to shut*

coepī, *I began*

cōgitō, -āre, -āvī, -ātus, *to think, consider*

cōnor, -ārī, -ātus sum, *to try*

cōnsīdō, cōnsīdere, cōnsēdī, *to sit down*

convīva, -ae, m., *guest (at a banquet)*

convīvium, -ī, n., *feast, banquet*

corōna, -ae, f., *garland, crown*

corpus, corporis, n., *body*

creō, -āre, -āvī, -ātus, *to appoint, create, make*

crūdēlis, -is, -e, *cruel*

crūdēlitās, crūdēlitātis, f., *cruelty*

cubiculum, -ī, n., *bedroom*

cum, prep. + abl., *with*

cum, conj., *when, since, whenever*

cupiō, cupere, cupīvī, cupītus, *to desire, want*

Cūr . . . ? *Why . . . ?*
currō, currere, cucurrī, cursūrus, *to run*
custōdiō, -īre, -īvī, -ītus, *to guard*

D

dē, prep. + abl., *down from, from, concerning, about*
dēbeō, -ēre, -uī, -itus, *to owe;* + infin., *ought*
dēfessus, -a, -um, *tired*
deinde, adv., *then, next*
dēlectō, -āre, -āvī, -ātus, *to delight, amuse, please*
dēmittō, dēmittere, dēmīsī, dēmissus, *to let down, lower*
dēmōnstrō, -āre, -āvī, -ātus, *to show*
dēscendō, dēscendere, dēscendī, dēscēnsūrus, *to come/go down, climb down*
deus, -ī, nom. pl., **dī,** dat., abl. pl., **dīs,** m., *god*
dīcō, dīcere, dīxī, dictus, *to say, tell*
diēs, diēī, m., *day*
dīligenter, adv., *carefully*
discipulus, -ī, m., *pupil*
discō, discere, didicī, *to learn*
dō, dare, dedī, datus, *to give*
domī, *at home*
dūcō, dūcere, dūxī, ductus, *to lead, take, bring*
dum, conj., *while, as long as*
duo, duae, duo, *two*

E

ēbrius, -a, -um, *drunk*
effugiō, effugere, effūgī, *to flee, run away, escape*
ego, *I*
ēlegāns, ēlegantis, *elegant, tasteful*
ēmittō, ēmittere, ēmīsī, ēmissus, *to send out*
enim, conj., *for*
errō, -āre, -āvī, -ātūrus, *to wander, be mistaken*
et, conj., *and, also*
etiam, adv., *also, even*
excipiō, excipere, excēpī, exceptus, *to welcome, receive, catch*
excitō, -āre, -āvī, -ātus, *to rouse, wake (someone) up*
exclāmō, -āre, -āvī, -ātus, *to exclaim, shout out*

exeō, exīre, exiī or **exīvī, exitūrus,** irreg., *to go out*
exstinguō, exstinguere, exstīnxī, exstīnctus, *to put out, extinguish*
extrā, prep. + acc., *outside*
extrahō, extrahere, extrāxī, extractus, *to drag out, take out*

F

facilis, -is, -e, *easy*
faciō, facere, fēcī, factus, *to make, do*
familia, -ae, f., *family, household*
fēlīx, fēlīcis, *lucky, happy, fortunate*
ferō, ferre, tulī, lātus, irreg., *to bring, carry, bear*
fīō, fierī, factus sum, irreg., *to become, be made, be done, happen*
flammeum, -ī, n., *orange (bridal) veil*
forte, adv., *by chance*
fortis, -is, -e, *brave, strong, mighty*
frīgidus, -a, -um, *cold*
frōns, frontis, gen. pl., **frontium,** f., *forehead*
fūrtim, adv., *stealthily*

G

gaudeō, gaudēre, gavīsus sum, *to be glad, rejoice*
gaudium, -ī, n., *joy*
gerō, gerere, gessī, gestus, *to wear; carry on, perform, do*
gladiātor, gladiātōris, m., *gladiator*
glōria, -ae, f., *fame, glory*
gravis, -is, -e, *heavy, serious*

H

habeō, -ēre, -uī, -itus, *to have, hold*
haereō, haerēre, haesī, haesūrus, *to stick*
hic, haec, hoc, *this, the latter*
homō, hominis, m., *man*
  hominēs, hominum, m. pl., *people*

I

iaceō, -ēre, -uī, -itūrus, *to lie, be lying down*
iam, adv., *now, already*
iānua, -ae, f., *door*
ibi, adv., *there*
īdem, eadem, idem, *the same*
igitur, conj., *therefore*
ille, illa, illud, *that; he, she, it; the former*
in, prep. + abl., *in, on, among*

in, prep. + acc., *into, against*
incendium, -ī, n., *fire*
incola, -ae, f., *inhabitant, tenant*
incrēdibiliter, adv., *in an unbelievable way*
inde, adv., *from there, then*
īnfirmus, -a, -um, *weak, shaky, frail*
ingēns, ingentis, *huge*
inquam, *I say*
    inquit, *(he/she) says, said*
inter, prep. + acc., *between, among*
intrō, -āre, -āvī, -ātus, *to enter, go into*
invītō, -āre, -āvī, -ātus, *to invite*
ipse, ipsa, ipsum, *himself, herself, itself,*
    themselves, very
īrātus, -a, -um, *angry*
is, ea, id, *he, she, it; this, that*
ita, adv., *thus, so, in this way, in such a way*
itaque, adv., *and so, therefore*
iubeō, iubēre, iussī, iussus, *to order, bid*
iungō, iungere, iūnxī, iūnctus, *to join*

L

labor, labōris, m., *work, toil*
lāna, -ae, f., *wool*
lavō, lavāre, lāvī, lautus, *to wash*
licet, licēre, licuit + dat., *it is allowed*
līmen, līminis, n., *threshold, doorway*
lingua, -ae, f., *tongue, language*
locus, -ī, m.; n. in pl., *place*
longus, -a, -um, *long*
lūdus, -ī, m., *game, school*
lūx, lūcis, f., *light*

M

magister, magistrī, m., *schoolmaster,*
    master
magnificus, -a, -um, *magnificent*
magnus, -a, -um, *great, big, large, loud*
    (voice)
malus, -a, -um, *bad, evil*
manus, -ūs, f., *hand, band (of men)*
marītus, -ī, m., *husband*
mātrōna, -ae, f., *married woman*
maximē, adv., *very much, very, most*
melior, melior, melius, gen., **meliōris**,
    better
meus, -a, -um, *my, mine*
minor, minor, minus, gen., **minōris**,
    smaller
miser, misera, miserum, *unhappy,*
    miserable, wretched
miserābilis, -is, -e, *miserable, wretched*

mittō, mittere, mīsī, missus, *to send, let*
    go
modo, adv., *only*
moneō, -ēre, -uī, -itus, *to advise, warn*
morior, morī, mortuus sum, *to die*
mōs, mōris, m., *custom*
mox, adv., *soon, presently*
multus, -a, -um, *much;* pl., *many*
    multum, adv., *much, long*
mūrus, -ī, m., *wall*

N

nam, conj., *for*
natō, -āre, -āvī, -ātūrus, *to swim*
nē . . . quidem, adv., *not even*
nec, conj., *and . . . not*
necesse, adv. or indecl. adj., *necessary*
neglegenter, adv., *carelessly*
neglegentia, -ae, f., *carelessness*
nēmō, nēminis, m./f., *no one*
neque, conj., *and . . . not*
nesciō, -īre, -īvī, -ītus, *to be ignorant, not*
    to know
nihil, *nothing*
    nīl, *nothing*
nisi, conj., *unless, if . . . not, except*
nōlō, nōlle, nōluī, irreg., *to be unwilling,*
    not to wish, refuse
nōn, adv., *not*
nōnnumquam, adv., *sometimes*
nōs, *we, us*
nox, noctis, gen. pl., **noctium**, f., *night*
nūllus, -a, -um, *no, none*
Num . . . ? adv., *Surely . . . not . . . ?*
    (introduces a question that expects
    the answer "no")
nunc, adv., *now*
nūpta, -ae, f., *bride*

O

occurrō, occurrere, occurrī, occursūrus
    + dat., *to meet*
oculus, -ī, m., *eye*
omnis, -is, -e, *all, the whole, every, each*
oppressus, -a, -um, *overcome, crushed*
optimus, -a, -um, *best, very good, excellent*
ōrātor, ōrātōris, m., *orator, speaker*
ōs, ōris, n., *mouth, face, expression*
ostendō, ostendere, ostendī, ostentus,
    to show, point out

P

parātus, -a, -um, *ready, prepared*
parēns, parentis, m./f., *parent*
pars, partis, gen. pl., **partium**, f., *part, direction, region*
paucī, -ae, -a, *few*
per, prep. + acc., *through, along, over*
percutiō, percutere, percussī, percussus, *to strike*
persuādeō, persuādēre, persuāsī, persuāsus, *to make something* (acc.) *agreeable to someone* (dat.), *to persuade someone of something; to persuade someone* (dat.)
perterritus, -a, -um, *frightened, terrified*
pēs, pedis, m., *foot*
petō, petere, petīvī, petītus, *to look for, seek, head for, aim at, attack*
piscīna, -ae, f., *fishpond*
placeō, -ēre, -uī + dat., *to please*
plūs, plūris, n., *more*
pōnō, pōnere, posuī, positus, *to put, place*
populus, -ī, m., *people*
porta, -ae, f., *gate*
possum, posse, potuī, irreg., *to be able; I can*
postis, postis, gen. pl., **postium**, m., *door-post*
praetereā, adv., *besides, too, moreover*
prīmus, -a, -um, *first*
prīnceps, prīncipis, m., *emperor, leader, leading citizen*
prōcēdō, prōcēdere, prōcessī, prōcessūrus, *to go forward*
propinquus, -ī, m., *relative*
propter, prep. + acc., *on account of, because of*
prūdēns, prūdentis, *wise, sensible*
puer, puerī, m., *boy*
pugna, -ae, f., *fight, battle, gladiatorial match*
pulcher, pulchra, pulchrum, *beautiful, pretty, handsome*

Q

quaerō, quaerere, quaesīvī, quaesītus, *to seek, look for, ask (for)*
quam, adv., *than, as*
quamquam, conj., *although*
-que, enclitic conj., *and*
quī, quae, quod, *who, which, that*

Quī . . . ? Quae . . . ? Quod . . . ? *What . . . ? Which . . . ?*
quīdam, quaedam, quoddam, *a certain*
quiēs, quiētis, f., *rest*
Quis . . . ? Quid . . . ? *Who . . . ? What . . . ?*
quō, adv., *there, to that place*
quod, conj., *because;* with verbs of feeling, *that*
Quōmodo . . . ? adv., *In what way . . . ? How . . . ?*
quoque, adv., *also*

R

rēctus, -a, -um, *right, proper, upright*
redeō, redīre, rediī or **redīvī, reditūrus**, irreg., *to return, go back*
relinquō, relinquere, relīquī, relictus, *to leave behind*
rēs, reī, f., *thing, matter, affair, situation*
resistō, resistere, restitī + dat., *to resist*
respondeō, respondēre, respondī, respōnsūrus, *to reply*
rīsus, -ūs, m., *laughter, laugh, smile*
rogō, -āre, -āvī, -ātus, *to ask*
Rōma, -ae, f., *Rome*
Rōmānus, -a, -um, *Roman*
rūsticus, -a, -um, *of or belonging to the country or country estate*

S

saepe, adv., *often*
sanguis, sanguinis, m., *blood*
scelus, sceleris, n., *crime*
sē, *himself, herself, oneself, itself, themselves*
sed, conj., *but*
semper, adv., *always*
septem, *seven*
servō, -āre, -āvī, -ātus, *to save, protect*
sī, conj., *if*
sīc, adv., *thus, so, in this way*
signum, -ī, n., *signal, sign*
silva, -ae, f., *woods*
similis, -is, -e + dat., *similar (to), like*
simul, adv., *together, at the same time*
simulō, -āre, -āvī, -ātus, *to pretend*
sine, prep. + abl., *without*
soleō, solēre, solitus sum + infin., *to be accustomed (to), be in the habit of*
sōlus, -a, -um, *alone*
somnus, -ī, m., *sleep*
spectāculum, -ī, n., *sight, spectacle*

spectō, -āre, -āvī, -ātus, *to watch, look at*
statim, adv., *immediately*
stō, stāre, stetī, statūrus, *to stand*
studium, -ī, n., *enthusiasm, study*
sum, esse, fuī, futūrus, irreg., *to be*
superō, -āre, -āvī, -ātus, *to overcome,*
    defeat
suprā, prep. + acc., *above*
suus, -a, -um, *his, her, one's, its, their*
    (own)

T
taberna, -ae, f., *shop*
tablīnum, -ī, n., *study*
taeda, -ae, f., *torch*
tālia, n. pl., *such things*
tam, adv., *so*
tamen, adv., *however, nevertheless*
tamquam, conj., *just as if*
tantum, adv., *only*
tantus, -a, -um, *so great*
temptō, -āre, -āvī, -ātus, *to try*
tempus, temporis, n., *time*
tergum, -ī, n., *back, rear*
timeō, -ēre, -uī, *to fear, be afraid of/to*
timidus, -a, -um, *afraid, fearful, timid*
tōtus, -a, -um, *all, the whole*
trahō, trahere, trāxī, tractus, *to drag, pull*
tremō, tremere, tremuī, *to tremble*
trīstis, -is, -e, *sad*
tū, *you* (sing.)
tum, adv., *at that moment, then*
tumultus, -ūs, m., *uproar, commotion*
turba, -ae, f., *crowd, mob, confusion*
tuus, -a, -um, *your* (sing.)

U
ubi, adv., conj., *where, when*
umquam, adv., *ever*
Unde . . . ? adv., *From where . . . ?*
unde, adv., *from where*
ūnus, -a, -um, *one*
urbs, urbis, gen. pl., urbium, f., *city*
ut, conj. + indicative, *as,*
    when
ut, conj. + subjunctive, *so*
    that, that, to

V
vehementer, adv., *very much, violently,*
    hard, insistently
veniō, venīre, vēnī, ventūrus, *to come*
verbum, -ī, n., *word, verb*
vērus, -a, -um, *true*
    vērō, adv., *truly, really, indeed*
vestīmenta, -ōrum, n. pl., *clothes*
via, -ae, f., *road, street*
videō, vidēre, vīdī, vīsus, *to see*
vigilō, -āre, -āvī, -ātūrus, *to stay awake*
vincō, vincere, vīcī, victus, *to conquer,*
    win
vīnum, -ī, n., *wine*
vir, virī, m., *man*
vīs, acc., vim, abl., vī, f., *force*
vītō, -āre, -āvī, -ātus, *to avoid*
vīvō, vīvere, vīxī, vīctūrus, *to live*
vocō, -āre, -āvī, -ātus, *to call, invite*
volō, velle, voluī, irreg., *to wish, want, be*
    willing
voluptās, voluptātis, f., *pleasure, delight*
vōs, *you* (pl.)
vulnus, vulneris, n., *wound*
vultus, -ūs, f., *face, expression*